LEAN SIX SIGMA FOR BEGINNERS

A Quickstart Beginner's Guide To Lean Six Sigma

G. Harver

3rd EDITION

Free bonus inside

Table of Contents

Introduction

Chances are you have heard of the Lean Six Sigma method of management. Most people have. Unfortunately, the different management styles that people are used to do not involve the employees themselves in a positive manner. Rather, they are models that seek to have the employee toe the line and do minimal thinking, if any. Yet that same employee is the one closest to where the action is on a consistent basis.

In this book, you will learn how to involve every participant in the organization in the organization's processes, so that each of them feels responsible for the success of the organization. You will also learn the best means to cut down on waste, which is another way of showing you how to minimize costs as you improve performance. One of the most desired characteristics of the Lean Six Sigma methodology is how specific it is. Every stage of every process is supported by well assembled data. For that reason, you are able to act decisively without having to worry about other considerations that may introduce biases or prejudices.

Great entrepreneurs like Henry Ford pioneered the Lean Six Sigma mode of management, and they grew to make a mark in the world. That is enough evidence that you can reach your potential in revenue earnings, and lead the pack in your industry by applying the essentials of Lean Six Sigma in their modern form. This book shows you how you can get a select number of staff trained and then use them to pioneer change in your institution. It takes you through the main training stages, showing you the importance of certification in this area. You will even be able to see how marketable professionals who are versed in the workings of Lean Six Sigma are. This book even makes mention of big multinationals who continue to hire black belts and other certified persons. You will be able to see the most common jobs that call for Lean Six Sigma certification with a top of the range salary.

In this book, you can learn how to improve performance, not just in the business sector, but also in the professional arena. You will be able to see how you can streamline systems in a way that services flow efficiently and clients feel satisfied to the extent of giving your organization a vote of confidence. In fact, the book goes a step further and shows you how possible it is to improve processes within government as well, improving staff performance while lowering government expenditure. And you can even see how making the health sector efficient, in turn, impacts the wider society with things like reduced sick leaves and so on.

When you read this book, you will see that it is possible, in all areas of operation, to have a great working environment and still keep costs low and yields high. You will also appreciate the importance of Lean Six Sigma, especially considering it is an area that is already tested internationally, and a credible certification process put in place. It is now your opportunity to see how much potential you are yet to explore, by taking up the Lean Six Sigma approach that has propelled many companies to the top, becoming pace setters in their respective industries.

Happy reading and best wishes as you watch your expenses drop, your performance improve and your profits shoot up!

Chapter 1:
What, exactly, is Lean Six Sigma?

Excuse me, but whatever Lean Six Sigma happens to be, you will agree it cannot be bulky because we are clearly told it is lean. Some things are that obvious – and that is a good starting point. It cannot also carry fluff and unnecessary baggage with it. That is what lean connotes, isn't it? So, we have bagged those initial marks; let us now find out what Six Sigma then is.

Simply put, Six Sigma is a method of working where you focus on minimizing wastage in whatever it is that you are doing. We have in mind the service sector; the manufacturing sector; and even the trading sector. Six Sigma helps you monitor, through observed data, how well you are doing. What you do in Six Sigma is analyze the data within your project and establish the degree of poor performance – and that is what you work on reducing.

Surely, you understand what we are essentially saying. For example, if you happen to be manufacturing a brand of alcoholic drinks, there is no way you will anticipate sending out to the market some cartons with empty bottles well corked. This is because your plan is not to short-change your customers and chase them away, but to supply them with cartons of full bottles of the drink. You do not also want to send out some batches with lower alcohol levels than stated on the label. Six Sigma is basically that – no complicated stuff.

If you are running a salon, you want your clients to leave your parlor with their heads looking like the picture you both agreed on – or maybe close. And if your role is to supply materials to a manufacturing entity, you cannot surely afford to be that notorious supplier costing your customers hours upon hours of downtime because of your unreliable deliveries. You need to have set timelines within which to make deliveries after receiving the orders.

In short, Lean Six Sigma calls for systems whose performance can be measured. And after gauging your performance against what is expected, you deduce where losses are occurring in terms of wasted inputs and so on; and then you correct that.

So what are the guidelines in Six Sigma?

- First of all, you need to know what you would like to achieve: your intended specifications

- Then you need to measure the results of your performance at every stage of the process. For purposes of credible assessment, you need to then get the average of various results that you get over a set period of time, and that is the figure you then take as your mean for purposes of calculations.

Those two – your intended results and your actual mean results – must be as close as possible for you to speak of efficiency and impressive performance. The wider the variation between those two levels, the worse you are performing. In short, you do not want to deviate from what you planned with a big margin. You want to be as close as possible to what you initially planned. And you know what they call such kind of discrepancies? Well, they are called deviations. And that is because you are deviating from the planned results. You are deviating from the best way of doing things; the reason your performance is not optimum.

Your Expectations for Lean Six Sigma

At the end of the day, what you seek to achieve when you introduce this methodology of doing things into your organization is:

Alignment of projects with the organization's strategic objectives

This you do by having clearly defined roles for everyone involved and having set protocols for measurements

Objective assessment of processes

You want to know how ready the processes are to deliver the required output at the quality anticipated – and that is as close as possible to excellence

Modification or even overhaul of existing inefficient processes

The extent to which this is done, of course, is determined by the results of the processes assessment.

But how do we use Six Sigma to evaluate performance?

That is easy – always is, when you are using specific data and clear procedure. To help you gauge if you are doing well using the Six Sigma method, you are given an accepted deviation against which to compare your success. As such, if your mean performance is within the accepted standard deviation from your set goal, you can give yourself a pat on the back. Your performance, whether in production; in trade; or even in service provision can be termed good.

But why, really, can you not be even closer to your goal than that; not deviating at all? What would happen if you smelt or even touched success; or the best performance possible? Would you not be the best rated in your industry? Would you not be reaping the most profits that you could? Would you also not have a well-oiled system where things work whether you are around supervising or not?

Essentially, you would be utilizing every bit of input to its optimum and incurring no losses or waste. The implication of such efficiency is that every input and every effort contributes directly and unmistakably to revenue creation. No input is in excess and none is redundant. In the same vein, inputs are not insufficient in a manner to cause downtime or bottlenecks. Lean Six Sigma is about smooth running processes utilizing only inputs that are relevant and necessary to produce the desired results as per plan.

That is the working of Lean Six Sigma when implemented by knowledgeable people: getting rid of the sticky stuff that lines the performance passage slowing it down. Think of the doctor's recommendation as far as your heart is concerned – clear the bad cholesterol that lines up your arteries, and if there is plaque do the same; and the blood will serve your body like you are just beginning your youth. That is what the call is in all spheres of life. You need to clear anything that slows down your performance.

Now, you will agree that you need to know exactly what this sticky stuff is in order to know what kind of brush to use to get rid of it. It is even important, before then, to ascertain if it is cleanable in the first place, because if it is not, a major decision will need to be made regarding the viability of the whole project.

Here are the eight categories of waste that you need to set your eyes on:

- Downtime

- Overproduction

- Waiting

- Non utilized talent

- Transportation

- Inventory

- Motion

- Extra processing

Shorten it as DOWNTIME, and you will not forget it.

Wow! That technical sounding term – Lean Six Sigma – boils down to bringing down DOWNTIME as far as humanly possible...? It surely does; even when what is humanly possible involves using machinery and technical knowhow. It is essentially about making best use of resources at your disposal, and reducing redundancy all round.

For those who know nothing about reducing DOWNTIME, waste within an organization becomes like a disease or a cultural weakness. Individuals do not tie their wasteful actions to the organization's end results. And that is what Lean Six Sigma seeks to clean up. Every move and every piece of resource has an impact on the organization's end results, and this is what every employee is made to appreciate when working within Lean Six Sigma projects. And since the processes are data based and all evaluations are clear at every stage, it is easy for individuals concerned to appreciate when they are doing well for the company and when they are doing the organization disservice through inefficiencies.

Whereas the Lean Six Sigma way of working may seem to keep everyone on their toes, once they get the hang of it, it becomes a morale booster as great performers stand out through measurable results.

Chapter 2:
How Lean Six Sigma Works on a Daily Basis

Hey! How much profit would you like? Really, that is not a question you expect to hear from anyone who calls you an entrepreneur – not at all. So let us agree we call such a question redundant. Or maybe you prefer to call it rhetorical. The reality is that you and I want as much profit as we can make, otherwise we would just be whiling away time on some warm beach and putting in an hour or so a week to attend to business.

But entrepreneurs are in the business of maximizing profits. That is why we are trying to understand this method that has propelled many a business to the top in their respective industries. Maybe at this juncture you need to know that the concept of Six Sigma began with Motorola where they wanted nothing but perfection for their product. Otherwise, what would you call aiming at 99.99966% perfection, which is what Motorola did? Some people would call that going nuts, but really, do you not think there is a chance of landing on the moon if you aimed for the sun? And that way, you will still be leading the pack.

So does Lean Six Sigma aim for quality?

Let us begin by explaining that Motorola initiated the Six Sigma method of business management back in 1986 and it targeted quality of products. Now we have taken up that method of management to ensure that we achieve great financial strides; and that, we cannot do, without taking quality on a serious note. How then are we carrying out business today, you may wonder? Well, we are aiming at raising the level of both quality and quantity.

Have we just said quantity? You sure got that right. True, Motorola may have found success in quality, but believe you me, for best performance and highest profits, it is imperative that you have both quality and quantity; and quantity comes with speed of production or performance. That is why Six Sigma is only part of our business management method; we have Lean to complete it.

Mark you, even in calculating profits, they normally begin with the sales turnover figure. If you sold the best car in the world but sold only one unit, we could call you a perfectionist; a philanthropist; or something of the sort, but nothing close to a business guru. This is essentially because, so as to maximize profits, you need both quality and quantity at their optimum.

This is how Lean Six Sigma takes care of DOWNTIME (those waste elements) on a daily basis:

Defects

This is part of the wastage that you incur from certain inefficiencies including:

- Use of inaccurate information

- Applying poor workmanship which leads to revision of jobs

- Unwarranted wear and tear

Overproduction

This is in reference to waste that comes about because you bring out your service or product when it is least needed. Such an instance is when you bring your product out long before its time. And so there are few people ready to consume it. Ever heard of the principle of supply and demand? Well, if, for example, you supply us ice-cream in winter, how many people do you expect to sell to? If it is only a handful, then you can be sure that your excessive supply compared to extremely low demand is bound to cause a dip in price. Where, then, would you get high profits from? Surely you will even be lucky to break even.

Then there is the outright overproduction. If, for example, you fill your farm with tomatoes in an area that has no processing plant, do you not see you are going to flood the market with your product at its prime, because we can consume only this much? You can see clearly that whatever the amount we consume, it has a limit. So, beyond that, it is all a waste.

Waiting

How many times have you heard that time is money? Yet because you are preoccupied with the anxiety of missing the bus; the boss shouting; being caught up in the traffic jam; and such other unpleasant experiences, you fail to see the bigger picture. Lean Six Sigma gets you to work within the larger picture, and that makes you see the impact that lost time has on performance, and ultimately, success. For example:

- How many man hours do you pay for in terms of wages whereas your employees were just sitting and chatting with no materials to work with?

11

- How many orders do you lose for failing to make deliveries in time?

- How many business deals do you lose in millions of dollars for keeping potential stakeholders waiting?

There is a lot you could improve in your business just by adhering to timelines; and also by streamlining the existing systems so that every task is performed at its appropriate time.

Non utilized talent

Once upon a time they used to speak of division of labor. That has its advantages alright – but how far do you think you can go if you cannot allow your driver to carry a parcel from the company to one of the clients you are going to have a chat with, just because you are an executive who is driven in an executive car by an executive driver? Surely, these are appearances you are trying to keep and they do not contribute to maximizing profits for your organization. If your driver can fill in a delivery book, why not kill two birds with the same proverbial stone? He drives you alright but then he also delivers the parcel for your organization. Your check might even come earlier than if you waited for the company messenger to deliver the same parcel, say, a week later.

How about paying an accountant yet you allocate him or her duties to handle petty cash day in day out? Are you kidding? What part of the petty cash handling is sufficient to pay an accountant? Yet, you are not ready to engage the accountant in policy making even where everything is about profit making... Something is amiss here, and sooner or later it shows up in the final results – business performance; amount of profit made.

Transportation

Have you ever observed movements taking place in a working environment and you wondered if there was some fun involved and you were the only one in the dark? Someone goes upstairs and comes down with a hammer and is told a hammer is not fit for the job. He retraces steps back upstairs and this time comes down with a pair of magnificent pliers. This pair also does not accomplish the job and the guy has to return upstairs for a third time. And before you can find out if this time the implement being brought down will be fitting for the job at hand, you feel like spitting out a number of questions:

- Does the person doing the sending actually appreciate what the job entails?

- Is the person being sent familiar with the different implements used?

- Do the workers here plan their work in advance to know what they need?

- Does this place have a procurement system or people just pick anything from anywhere anytime?

All these are questions, which, if properly addressed would reduce time spent on wasteful movement of items.

And the scenario could even be more ridiculously wasteful. Visualize the transportation cost involved when this kind of inefficiency involves movement of materials, and even finished product, from a go-down far off somewhere. Fuel is unnecessarily used for the delivery trucks and time is wasted by all personnel involved because it does not amount to increased output, quality or even efficiency.

Inventory

Surely if you are going to import products, may they be in amounts that you can clear from the airport in good time, and amounts that you can offload and store in secure places in good time. But if your order arrives in truckloads, and you do not have enough space for them all, the time it takes you to look for additional storage can cost you time and also losses. Who says your goods cannot be stolen in the meantime since you had not planned for extra security? Who says they cannot be spoilt if they are dumped in the open as you look for storage?

So, ideally, you need to have enough hands to offload your inventory as it comes in, and enough capacity to process any materials you order from wherever it is. Could you imagine a professional chef – no, chefs seem to be more sensitive – a caterer ordering for packets of sausages for a big occasion only to realize he is two or three days early? Surely, unless you always have idle capacity in your cold storage, you could find yourself facing huge wastage in form of stale sausages. The point is: inventory needs to be processed as it arrives without undue delay.

Motion

Ah... oh... hey... All these are sounds we often make when our mind is wondering where to transit to. In short, I am through with this process and I am not sure where my services are required next. I therefore murmur absent mindedly as I move aimlessly. That is also the time to interrupt those who are busy in a bid to make yourself relevant. *What is it you are engaged in? You actually mean you are here? Don't tell me you are still busy...* Asking those redundant questions does not constitute being productive. The fact is that you are just wasting time walking here, there and everywhere; in the process, you are adversely influencing other people towards your bandwagon. That is why you need to minimize aimless movements during working time. You need to appreciate that idle movements do not constitute leisure. Scheduled leisure time is helpful but idling about is not.

Extra processing

Have you ever witnessed a carpenter sanding wood? It is fascinating to see how smooth the wood becomes with every movement. But if there is Formica to be fixed on the piece of wood, that piece of wood may not need sanding as much as it would if it was to have varnish. So, beyond a certain point, you would be wasting time and sandpaper working on the wood.

In short, if you are to work optimally, give the required quality; do not stretch yourself beyond your set standards. After all, who cares if not the person who gave you the specifications? In any case, if time comes when your client needs higher standards, those will come with higher pricing – or are you not in business? All this is in a bid to reduce the cost of inputs, keeping in mind that you expect a specific level of revenues from your output. You are, therefore, trying to ensure that you do not overload your input side lest it eats into your profits.

Chapter 3:
Beneficiaries of Lean Six Sigma

Do you think any organization or enterprise is too big or too tiny to cut down on waste and increase profits? Obviously, no – every organization is faced with situations of scarce resources and bigger revenue figures in their strategic plans, and so they would be glad to be part of Lean Six Sigma, a process that is geared towards reducing costs and increasing revenue. In short, size does not matter when it comes to the capacity to handle benefits of Lean Six Sigma.

In any case, any resources saved would go a long way into helping small or even medium size enterprises:

- Add a new product or even service to their offers or even improve existing products, services or even systems

- Expand workforce

- A lot more improvements

Here are some of the beneficiaries of Lean Six Sigma

Employees

Considering that employees are the ones in the midst of the action, whether the organization is moving downhill or up in profit making, it actually motivates them when they are actively involved in identifying the organization's shortcomings and devising ways of rectifying them. Therefore, the participatory nature of Lean Six Sigma makes the employees feel valued and as such leaves them with the feeling of ownership as far as implementation of changes goes. And even when the employees are faced with challenging processes, the fact that they already feel accountable keeps them determined and happy to be part of the challenge.

The health sector

Have you realized you have fewer requests for sick off as an employer when your employees are happy? That is a pointer that with many organizations implementing the Lean Six Sigma management style, health facilities are bound to experience less pressure. At the same time, it means that the efficiency that comes with Lean Six Sigma is bound to have patients enjoy better services; the aged more quality time with their minders; and, definitely, health workers spending less time dealing with unnecessary paperwork and such matters that do not impact on quality. So, we have higher quality services and fewer resources injected into mundane and unnecessary chores.

Technology

The technology sector is an obvious beneficiary of Lean Six Sigma in that more technology is going to be utilized the more evidence continues to come out that technology has a lot to do with increasing efficiency. With manufacturers being able to produce items of high standard and lower defect count, people are bound to be attracted into investing more in technology.

Financial sector

There is less time spent enrolling new customers when you have Lean Six Sigma in place. Even the time it takes to deliver services to customers is greatly reduced and that means attracting more customers while retaining the old ones. That, definitely, points to guaranteed continuity and expansion of your income stream; and increased financial activity just coming from the spillover effect.

Every industry

What this essentially means is that whatever industry you are in, you will find it important to put in place means of earning profits, minimizing cost, or both. So, Lean Six Sigma is the efficiency tool for all irrespective of their industry.

And what makes Lean Six Sigma certification worthwhile?

For one, more and more companies are getting into the mode of hunting for anything and anyone progressive as far as profitability is concerned. And that is how Lean Six Sigma has gained popularity. And hence the rise in demand for qualified and certified people to lead and drive the process. Needless to say, without having worked with someone before, the only way you can be sure they are competent is if they can pass as duly certified. Today, you can actually see advertisements of companies seeking to nab people who have been certified as professionals in Lean Six Sigma. Among the companies that have led the way is UnitedHealth Group; Honeywell; General Electric as well as Volkswagen.

Just so you know how marketable professionals holding Lean Six Sigma Certification are, here as some of some positions that companies in the Fortune 500 list have been seeking to fill:

Lean Six Sigma Consultant

This is a person who not only has the certification but also the experience in implementing Lean Six Sigma enough times to make him or her expert. This is actually the person who can foresee an obstacle before you get to it and guide you into avoiding it. In short, once you engage a Lean Six Sigma consultant, you can be sure of achieving your goals of improved performance and minimal loss much faster than otherwise.

Compliance Structural Engineer

This person is mostly required as a consultant in matters regarding Lean Six Sigma within the manufacturing sector.

Reliability Engineer

A reliability engineer is one who ensures that the assets being relied upon to make the processes a success do not lead to losses. He or she assesses the risk involved in their use and recommends the ones that keep the losses to a minimum. This is the same person who ensures that the asset life cycle is well managed.

Lead Manufacturing Engineer

This is the guy who sees to it that specifications are met. And here you are looking at the processes as well as the final product. From the stages of implementation all through in management of processes, the lead manufacturing engineer gives very important support to the team and all other stakeholders, to ensure that necessary standards are adhered to. This is the person who actually sees to it that quality of processes and products is audited within the organization itself.

Process Development Engineer

This is a person who specializes in designing production systems. In addition, this professional is also versed in managing teams and also on matters of quality assurance.

Business Process Analyst

This is that professional that you want analyzing the processes you are currently using and identifying their strengths and weaknesses with a view to making suggestions on improvement changes. Where automation is helpful, the business process analyst will let you know.

Operating System Specialist

This is someone who is great in researching; designing; developing and testing software; compilers; distribution networks; and a lot more to do with operating systems. Of course, as you may appreciate, a poor operating system can only lead you to losses emanating from time lost and a lot more.

Data Scientist

This is simply a business intelligence person; your consultant in matters of data analysis – statistics that ultimately help to sharpen your organization's competitive edge.

Senior IT Project Manager

This professional bears the responsibility of planning; organizing; leading; as well as controlling your Lean Six Sigma project in matters of information technology as efficiently and as effectively as humanly possible. This role is pivotal to the success of the whole organization.

Project Engineer

This is the professional you need for coordination in order to have your project running well. He or she leads your technical team to work in tandem with the project management team. In fact, many organizations want to have their project engineer doubling as their project manager.

Warehouse Operations Manager

This is the professional who drives efficiency on the operations of distribution centers – both industrial and warehousing. All inbound activities linked to receiving as well as storing goods; management of inventory as well as related claims is all the business of this professional. And that is not all. Even similar activities relating to overseas activities are on the Warehouse Operation Manager's plate.

Director, Performance Excellence

This professional is at the top of the management hierarchy when it comes to matters of project management; strategic implementation of plans and processes; and ensuring that whatever goes on under the project is in proper alignment to the values of the organization; its mission as well as vision.

Chapter 4:
Salaries Associated With Lean Six Sigma

You do not get vacancies being filled by the likes of GE and imagine the salary could be low. Yet the positions linked with Lean Six Sigma have the element of uniqueness and rarity, that making them even more marketable. So, if anyone had any doubt about the value attached to qualifications of Lean Six Sigma, they are about the erase them after going through the salary indications:

- It is said that if you are a Green Belt professional, your salary will, very likely, be higher than some other professional from the same field who does not have Lean Six Sigma certification. In fact, the figure given as premium for the Lean Six Sigma professional is 42%. Here we are saying that if you are an engineer with Salary X, when you get the Green Belt certification your market value will soar and your salary offer is likely to be 142X% of what you were earning before.

- Salary for Green Belts holders in the US is particularly high, and the average pay is something to the tune of $72,000 annually. For Black Belts, employers are known to put $98,000 on the table. Then when it comes to Master Black Belts, the salary for one individual comes to around $113,000 annually.

As such, you will find a good number of employees today enrolling for training in matters of Lean Six Sigma, as they strategically endeavor to make themselves, not only viable, but also highly marketable. Of course, for this you need to begin from the Yellow Belt certification.

How about salaries of trainers?

Surely a teacher must be better paid than the fresh graduate. In that case, trainers of belt holders earn relatively higher salaries. In fact, you should not be surprised to come across a Lean Six Sigma trainer earning something like $100,000 per annum. And you should also not lose sight of the fact that these trainers are often available for consultancy. The long and short of it is that when you get the necessary training and earn the relevant belt or belts, you find doors opening faster to let you take advantage of big time income generating opportunities.

Here are various industries where Black Belts are paid exemplary high salaries:

- Industries related with IT

- Industries associated with food and beverages

- Industries that deal with energy and utilities

Amongst all these industries, bear in mind that Master Black Belts are the highest paid.

Is the Lean Six Sigma training expensive?

Well, someone said many days and decades ago that should you want to have the real feel of cost, try to compare the implications of being ignorant with the impact of being well informed and skilled. With ignorance, you might find yourself paying through the nose and without prior planning. But with knowledge, you can reach sky high in performance as well as in imagination.

Anyway, brace yourself to pay something between $4,000 and $7,000. The consolation is that you will, very likely, be saving on transport cost and time as the belt certification courses are readily available on line. And also there are many employers who are ready to sponsor you if they find you competitive, focused and loyal to the business.

Chapter 5:
Things for CEOs to Note in Readiness to Implement Lean Six Sigma

That lean six sigma is for all types and all sizes of organizations

That it is not good to wait till you are making losses to begin thinking of implementing Lean Six Sigma. In short, do not await the following signs:

- Loss of revenues

- Loss of customers

- Loss of market share

And why is it so important that you do not wait till you are making losses? Simple – what happens when you are in danger? Like in this case you will be in danger of closing down your business or being relegated to a rank that nobody trusts much. When in danger, you begin to fight for mere survival. Yet the reason Lean Six Sigma is emphasized is to make improvements that will get to almost 100% perfection. So, although the methodology may help you salvage your company, it is not basically meant as a firefighting tool.

That Lean Six Sigma does not become redundant once you achieve success

Yes, as earlier stated, the methodology is meant to keep you on track; consistently evaluating processes, measuring achievements at every stage while at the same time measuring any losses and taking instant measures to return to perfection;

or, at least, near perfection. So you cannot afford to drop Lean Six Sigma just because you are now leading the pack or your shareholders are smiling all the way to the bank. You need it to maintain that success and the only way to do that is to keep following the basics of Lean Six Sigma.

In any case, you may be in the lead today but who says a competitor is not already employing the best brains versed in Lean Six Sigma to try and edge you out?

Lean Six Sigma is a structured approach to management

In short, you need to brace yourself for order and working systems and not just a structured system on paper. You need to give in to employee active participation even in terms of ideas because that is what Lean Six Sigma entails. The management system where employees are simply labor providers is kind of old school and will not help you minimize losses in your organization.

Decisions are, by default, made based on accurate data

In short, this is not a situation where you make decisions based on whims or emotions, or even your gut feeling. In Lean Six Sigma, everything is data based, and so you as the CEO, like your employees, is set for strict accountability. And you need to be aware that success in Lean Six Sigma is measured to the decimal and the margin of error that denotes success is very small.

Working under Lean Six Sigma calls for strict discipline

Did you know that once you get accustomed to acting in a disciplined manner you no longer need much effort to do it? This is what organizations that have achieved success via Lean Six Sigma are experiencing. Working with precision becomes part of them no matter the magnitude of the task. And as you can appreciate, the sum total of numerous well completed tasks is overall success of your project and exhilaration for the customer. What then would make a happy customer go anywhere else? You can only revel at the expansion of your customer base and smile at your bank account.

Acting with wit is not a luxury

Some of the demands Lean Six Sigma brings before you are not exactly alien. In fact most of them just call for you to employ your wit before making any and every move. That is why there is even a sequence of doing things – not because it is routine but because it is the most sensible thing to do. What comes to mind here?

- You surely want to understand a problem first before voicing a solution. That is only logical otherwise you may find yourself investing in so-called solutions that may be totally unhelpful.

- You then want to gather supporting data because as already mentioned elsewhere in this book, nothing within Lean Six Sigma management is without justification.

- Then follows the task of analyzing data

As you will understand, having data is not in itself good basis for changing processes. You need to analyze that data and look at what it means in the right perspective. You could analyze your raw data and realize that what you have as not-so-great performance is not as a result of systems but attitudes.

In such a case then, you definitely, will not need resource allocations for machinery, additional personnel and so on. What you may need is a vote for staff in-servicing and bonding; something that will change their attitude to one of working together and winning together.

- You then have the vital task of nailing the cause of the problem

Once you have had sufficient and relevant data and have analyzed it to see where the hitch lies, you need to trace the base of that problem. Without that, every attempt at problem solving will be superficial.

- Finally it is time to employ your wit to come up with a solution

Of course, in engaging your team, many possible solutions are likely to come up. But the question should always linger surrounding the viability of each one of those possible solutions. That is where your good wit should come in and give direction to the whole brainstorming. You need to settle for a solution – a corrective measure – that is viable.

Remember the reason your task has not achieved 100% success is one reason your organization is not performing at its best. And you have identified the weakness involved. Now you need a way to correct that weakness. And that corrective measure needs to bring forth performance that is sustainable.

Lean Six Sigma Projects take a process at a time

What is the logic? Well, if you implement different processes at the same time, how will you know which one helped you positively and to what degree? If one process is actually occasioning losses, how will you, again, tell which one it is that is doing that? In short, you will, definitely, be sabotaging your own efforts by implementing different processes concurrently; and you may find yourself reverting to acting on maybe's and likelihoods – nothing close to what Lean Six Sigma advocates.

Once you have been successful in implementing Lean Six Sigma, here is what you notice:

1. That you no longer embrace solutions to an imaginary or unexplained problem; and that you only embrace solutions after conclusive analysis of the data at hand.

2. That you now go for solutions that are bound to keep the relevant problems away. Those traditional methods of trial and error can really eat up your resources in a wasteful way; something you get to realize when you switch to Lean Six Sigma.

3. That you now direct your resources to processes that minimize inefficiencies. With data based identification of the problem; data based analysis of your possible solution; you are now spot on when it comes to investing in a long-term solution.

You need a reason that is compelling before you introduce Lean Six Sigma

If you do not do that and you pretty well know that your projects will require the participation and unequivocal support of everyone involved, you may not get much success. You need to have everyone in your organization buying into the idea of change.

You need to get your top management in your corner

From the onset, you need your colleagues at the top to understand what changes you have in mind. This is especially important because you do not want to have your senior managers feeling like they are losing power to ordinary employees. You need to give them a brief on what Lean Six Sigma is about and the wonders it has done to organizations that have embraced it.

And, of course, the fact that nothing changes in terms of where the buck stops on the overall and so, just as they are watched by the board for any missteps, so will they be credited with the organization's success when Lean Six Sigma gets the profits soaring.

A special vote for resources to facilitate Lean Six Sigma projects is necessary

Call a spade what it is so that you can prepare accordingly – avoid calling it a big spoon. If you think you will need to hire new personnel with knowledge of Lean Six Sigma and relevant experience, put that on the table when making your proposals at top level. If there are materials required, technology to be acquired or modified, or any other thing that will demand resources, let that be clear. Otherwise, a project can easily fail if it is not supported with the relevant resources. And then the organization ends up worse than it was in the first place.

Anyone with a stake in the organization needs to be on the loop

Take the case of a customer who has been casual with his or her specifications or even non-committal with timelines. These are the kind of customers who tell you the product can be delivered any time you have it ready, only for them to call in sounding an emergency. You cannot afford that with Lean Six Sigma. Product specifications need to be defined and clearly stated because that is the bench mark for the success of the process being used.

You need to set free members of your project team

What this means is that as CEO you need to remove anything that could frustrate the Lean Six Sigma projects. In this regard, you need to be ready to give members of your project teams a free hand in anything relating to the projects. The reason for this is that some of the action needed may sometimes fall on odd hours or require direct contact with clients.

So if every time a team member needs to do something they have to complete the conventional paper work and await approvals possibly from managers who have no idea when they are reporting to the office next, your project might be a disaster. So instead of boxing those members within the rules of the old system, you need to empower them in carrying out any initiatives they may deem fit for the success of the project.

It is crucial to set aside training funds

While training funds need not run into millions of dollars, you still need a couple of thousands to give your staff, particularly those who will be actively involved in projects, some insight as to what to expect of this new management style and methodology of working. Note that you have the option of bringing in an expert to give your staff in-house training.

Quality supersedes speed

Is it wrong to want to shine fast? No, it isn't. But it does not make economic sense to implement your Lean Six Sigma methodology fast without regard to other factors such as the readiness of your team or the availability of resources. If you are not on the same page as an organization while implementing Lean Six Sigma, you are off on the wrong footing. You could suffer sabotage or failure due to sheer ignorance.

If, however, you can achieve quality at a relatively slower pace, but it is quality that can be sustained within the limitations of your organization, you are fine. As CEO, you will be able to say with confidence that your new management style was worth the resources you put in.

You need to be receptive to feedback

Timeliness is of essence when working with Lean Six Sigma. As such, you need to break a few walls and let team members air their views freely. That is the only way you are going to learn things as they are. But if you insist on conventional protocol and formal language and format of feedback presentation, you may not learn enough authentic details to help you make effective decisions.

In any case, with a methodology like this that pushes for perfection, you need data and information that is as true and as real as it can be. After all, the reality always comes out in the results, when it is clear how far away from, or how close to, perfection your processes were.

Chapter 6:
Tying Lean to Six Sigma Method for Best Performance

Lean has everything to do with traveling light in a bid to facilitate speed. Traveling light means exactly that: taking with you only that which is absolutely necessary. The lean business management is what propelled Henry Ford of Ford Motor Company to great success, though at first Ford used the more crude management method of Taylor's that was deemed scientific. The main handicap with Taylor's method was inhibiting individual workers from being proactive. It, however, did some good because the boss did great thinking and exhaustive directing and monitoring, such that wastage was almost nil. But speed had to be introduced so that cars were produced en mass thus cutting down on unit costs.

How does Lean's speed help?

Look – the speed at which you can deliver what your customer needs determines how attached your customer will be to you. And what is the importance of customers in your life? Of course it is money. If you end up becoming social friends with them, it is a bonus. But what you aim at is attracting customers and retaining them for the longest time possible.

That is what Lean Six Sigma aims to achieve by meeting the customer's needs as fast as possible, while at the same time providing high quality service and product. It actually culminates in you providing value at an impressive speed; which in turn translates to you having a consistent inflow of cash. There, surely, cannot be a better way of guaranteeing great and steady business performance.

How do we measure performance using the Lean speed concept?

Keeping in mind that our success is determined by how well we keep our customers happy, we calculate the time that passes from when we begin working on the customer's order to the time we actually deliver. We call that Cycle time. The shorter that period is, the more successful we deem our performance to be.

If you take eternity, the customer will begin to sense danger, and the chance of not being satisfied with your work is pretty high. And that usually has good grounds. Is that it? Well, from practical experience it really is. Often when you delay delivering what the customer ordered, there is a list of things that may be wrong; and they include:

- Low morale on the part of your workforce

- The work being too complex for your firm

- Product defects discovered and are being corrected

- Team handling too many jobs at a time

- Lack of flexibility on the team to adjust to the demands of the customer

- Inefficient systems

In the customer's mind, any one of these shortcomings could have occurred and it is unlikely that you will be top of the list next time the customer wants a job done. Is your income flow thus guaranteed? The answer is no. Instead of concentrating on fulfilling orders you will be busy hunting for customers. That is no way to grow your business. You need to retain your current customers through continued efficiency, even as others are attracted to your performance.

What are we essentially saying about speed and efficiency?

We are essentially saying that you need to keep the customer happy and hopeful; you cannot afford to break the customer's faith in you. But even then, you must be realistic about your capacity and your mode of operation. If you are using a plant which costs you dearly to stop and restart within short spans, then you need to schedule your processes such that you do not have to literally stop the plant within short periods of operation.

Here are suitable measures for lean speed:

- Liaise with customers so that you know exactly when to start processing one customer's order and when to end it and take another customer's order without stopping your machines or having your workforce halting.

- Reduce the number of tasks your people do at the same time because it becomes more like attending to many pots at the same time. You spend too much time moving from one pot to the next, and ultimately one of them is likely to either boil over or burn. And that is some of the waste we are trying to avoid.

- Try and work towards making numerous small deliveries than huge batches that take forever and create anxiety on the part of the client. The important word here is not necessarily size but clearly, consistency. Supposing you are consistent in making your deliveries; you retain the customer's trust and your plant keeps running, and so you avoid burning fuel unnecessarily restarting the engine and motors every time. Can you see another advantage in early deliveries even when they are in batches? That with the delivery of the first batch, you get a chance to get feedback. To your advantage, if there is something the customer would rather you added, you then incorporate that in the subsequent batches.

- Have a rhythm – cadence. If you do, your customers are not going to ask when the next delivery will be – it will be obvious. And what a great working relationship! Your customer will not wish to leave and begin an uncertain relationship with another manufacturer or service provider.

- Avoid biting more than you can chew lest you lose trust with your clients. For instance, if you are a bottler and your bottling plant can produce a maximum of 20,000 bottles each single day, and you happen to have three brands to produce, why would you commit to supplying 50000 bottles of one brand every week to a customer? Are you not going to face hitches considering that customers for the other brands will also be on the queue waiting? The message simply is that you need to take orders according to your capacity.

At the end of the day, your short cycle time and customer satisfaction will have fulfilled what Lean Six Sigma seeks to achieve: minimum waste, best performance and high returns on investment.

Chapter 7: Actual Six Sigma Gauge

Minimum waste, best performance, high returns on investment... We have just said those are what Lean Six Sigma seeks to achieve. The question is: besides closing your organization's books of accounts with a higher figure than that of last year, how are you going to tell if your Lean Six Sigma project actually did what it was set to do?

Easy – with Lean Six Sigma, it is all specifics; no theories or stories. No biases or prejudices. No wishes – just realities. In fact, if you recall, every stage has its explicit results that are evaluated and monitored. Or how else do we get that average we talked about? Do you remember that average that you then compare to your standards and then determine to what extent you are deviating from what is expected?

Can we paint a practical situation for better understanding?

Here: you want to do well; 100% if you can. That means you want every piece of material that you sign out of the store or wherever the storage is to get utilized to the optimum. You do not want any wastage, no pilferage, and no poor usage. You want every minute that makes your working hours to be optimally spent. But the reality is that even when you have been as careful as can be, things do not always turn out perfect. In fact, in some situations achieving 100% would raise eyebrows.

Imagine a case where every liter of spirit you signed out in manufacture of an alcoholic beverage found its way into your final bottled product. What would you say if you were to consider that spirit evaporates to a certain degree? In short, here is a case where total efficiency in usage cannot be achieved. Yet since this small loss is anticipated, your technical explanation will be understandable. In manufacturing, they call it normal loss. The good thing is that for such scenarios, the percentage of normal loss, meaning, anticipated loss, is predetermined. In short, if the only loss in usage is that percentage, it will not be one of those things where the Project Champion seeks accountability from the Project Lead.

Easy assessment of a Lean Six Sigma Project

If you are one of those people who thank goodness every day for the invention of calculators; or possibly in your view the best creation of Microsoft is Excel, then you will breathe a sigh of relief to know that there is a simple way to calculate how badly you are doing at every stage of your project.

Yes – how badly. Remember Lean Six Sigma seeks to find out where you are messing with a view to rectifying that particular weakness. Again, this is nothing new but just the DOWNTIME you looked at earlier on – the weakness of Downtime; Overproduction; Waiting; Non utilized talent; Transportation; Inventory; Motion; and Extra processing. If you recall, it is in reducing these weaknesses that you come closer to your goal.

Suppose your plan is to produce 100 cakes but 5 of them get burnt. What percentage makes the bad cakes? Obviously, that is 5%. And what is the percentage that comprises the good cakes? That would be 95%. Without wanting to delve into the intricacies of how the initiators of this method made their final decision, it is important to state that the higher your percentage of success the higher your sigma level. That is exemplified by the level that Motorola was striving to achieve those years of beginning to implement this technique. They aimed at Sigma Level 6 and that represents 99.99966% success; and with only a loss of 0.00034%.

Of course in reality of business you are going to have items in millions and not hundreds the way it is in domestic production; and so, usually organizations talk of defects in a million units. And there is the level of capability and this one, just like the sigma level, reflects better performance the higher it is. And while the sigma level tops at 6, this one of capability tops at 2.

Below is a simple table that is referred to as Six Sigma Scale:

Sigma Level	Defects within a Million	Defects in %	Success (Yield) in %	Capability
1	691 462	69	31	0.33
2	308 538	31	69	0.67
3	66 807	6.7	93.3	1.00
4	6 210	0.62	99.38	1.33
5	233	0.023	99.977	1.67
6	3.4	0.00034	99.99966	2.00

Not to get lost in the figures, although with the scale you can really see where your process falls in terms of efficiency, let us summarize the key features of the Lean Six Sigma method of improving performance.

- This method focuses on the needs and expectations of the customer

- Assessments and decisions are based on actual data

- The ultimate goal is to reach the Six Sigma level, underlining the effectiveness of smart business management.

At the end of the day, you will have achieved very crucial components of business that contribute to overall success of your business both on short and long term basis. Close to mind are:

- Having content customers

- Reduced cycle period

- Reduced number of defects

Chapter 8:
Effective Application of Lean Six Sigma, including in Profession

Do you realize that there is a lot that can go right if you view your profession as your business? For one, you will begin to look at the people you are attending as your customers; customers that you value and not people at your mercy. And how does that change your behavior? Well, you begin to look into ways of serving them fast and effectively.

Do you now begin to see the overall impact on your career? The minute you begin to serve your clients fast is the minute you begin to save the institution's time. The minute you begin to offer high quality services is the minute you stamp your authority over those people you are serving, because inevitably, they will find themselves coming back in future for consultancy. So, you do not have to go out to the field and look for clients but instead they come to you en mass. If you are within the funded category of organizations, do you think you will need to do much convincing to attract more funding? Of course not – the flow of clients is bound to speak for you.

Is Lean Six Sigma helpful in times of appraisal?

If you have been practicing the Lean Six Sigma mode of management, and there is an appraisal underway, you are assured of either a promotion or upgrade without much ado. Obviously, whatever institution yours is, being upgraded from one level to another one above that is a big plus that comes with material benefits and prestige. If you are a service provider like a hospital, you easily become the institution of choice, a very invaluable position to be in.

How best can institutions implement Lean Six Sigma?

Good question this one is because theoretical knowledge will only help if it is implemented and actually implemented well. We begin with structures and systems. You need to know whom to entrust with what, otherwise, like some African cultures have it, *everyone's job is nobody's job*.

Create working teams

Build teams within your organization and teach them how Lean Six Sigma works

Organize so that each of your teams has a project that is clearly defined

Let your team members understand the correlation between every move that they make and the bottom line of the organization

Train key personnel

Identify key persons within your teams and train them in all aspects of statistics at an advanced level. That way, they will lead the team in documentation of data and also in data analysis. Surely you cannot tell the extent to which you are deviating from set standards unless you can calculate standard deviation with accuracy.

Use DMAIC to tackle problems

Oh... Oh – what does DMAIC stand for? Well, everything here is simple. You will simply be introducing an approach to problem solving; and that is what is dubbed DMAIC. And DMAIC is basically an acronym that helps you to remember the steps to take in tackling a problem. It goes thus:

- Define

- Measure

- Analyze

- Improve

- Control

Defining the Problem

You see, once you have defined exactly what the problem is, you are one step in the proper direction. Otherwise, as long as you have not put your finger on what is ailing your organization you could spend unlimited resources moving in circles and not correcting the situation.

Deliverables please... Here they are:

- The problem defining period is the phase during which the team comes into being. Born? No! Formed. And this requires careful evaluating of individuals so that you put people who are relevant and not redundant. Again you put together individuals who are compatible.

- Spelling out – in writing – the team charter. And here we have in mind that document that is to guide the Lean Six Sigma Team throughout the project period. It is like the constitution that guides a country but here they term it the backbone of the project.

- You establish and write down the customer's expectations

Here no assumptions are made. In Lean Six Sigma you cannot afford to say, for example, the customer wants bread and we know how bread is made so all we do is bake and deliver to the customer – no way! Workings here are customized. This particular customer may require bread with nuts or dates or anything else like that dotting the inside of the ready bread. The customer may even wish for a certain level of brownness. It is your business, your role, to listen to the customer and write down those specifications. Then adhere to them.

- Working parameters are set, including those of quality

Measuring the extent of the Problem

You need to measure how serious the problem is

Then once you measure the magnitude of the problem, you can begin to think of ways of handling it. If, for instance, you are faced with the problem of pilferage that is deep rooted, you may need to have an overhaul of your staff; an overhaul of your systems or actually both.

To be able to know what to lay your fingers on in restructuring, do you not think you need to have specifics to deal with? You have seen leaders rely on word of mouth and ended up making a whole fiasco of working changes. Other methods that do not seek to get measurable specifics are often influenced by personal feelings and attitudes and are hence subjective. And that is surely not the way to get you succeeding at a level of the over 90s percentile.

So where are those deliverables for measurement?

- Having a clear and effective plan of data collection

- Having a clear and uncomplicated way of system analysis

- Having reliable baseline data derived from your existing process

- Defining the operating processes

Analyzing the Problem

This is, of course, the analysis bit where you trace the steps to how you got off track in the first place and how you are actually doing currently. It is clear you are not doing very well today; the reason you still are not earning as much as you would like. You have not captured the market within your capacity and shareholders are not having a smile worth writing home about. In short, you are not very proud of your overall performance.

Now, you need to be clear if the problem is becoming more serious or it has reached a point of stagnation. That particular analysis also entails weighing your options because every move you make is bound to have an impact on the staff and possibly other stakeholders.

Improving the Situation

Once you have gone through these fundamental stages, it then gets to a point where you have to take action to rectify the situation. Here is where you need to be well focused because you could rub some people the wrong way while trying to improve the situation. But as they say, the finest gold just does not find itself glittering – rather, it absorbs a lot of heat in the process of refinement.

What you need to register is that with presumably an already existing system, you are only hoping to do better; and much better, of course because you are choosing a tested method of improving operations. But you are not certain that everyone in your organization is going to play ball. You do not know how effectively you will manage to put up a cohesive working team. In short, there cannot predict outcomes with certainty at this time. So, here is where you invoke caution and start by just a single project – call it a pilot project. You will be wiser along the way.

Talking deliverables:

- Propose a solution; and with it a clear cost-benefit analysis

- You have the project plan – execute it

- Present your proposals to the major stakeholders in this Project Management

Controlling the Situation

The final stage that deals with control calls for you to put measures in place to ensure that a similar problem does not recur. It is the time to ensure you have people to report progress and hitches in short regular intervals. It is also the time to make every team member know the extent of his or her responsibility. That is because if you leave the body of workers to feel like sheep whose work is just to follow, they are likely to watch as things go wrong, and sometimes even fuel a bad situation a little more.

If your problem is to do with high staff turnover, you may have to follow Henry Ford's step of raising wages as compared to his contemporaries and also pegging bonuses to individual contribution. That is attractive and motivating.

This is also the stage within which you ensure that the process changes you have made are not derailed – that you are on track at all stages of process implementation.

And the deliverables are...?

- Improvement of the implementation plan

- Diligent implementation of the process

- Actual process control

Do you feel anxious when trying something new? Bold as you may be, determined as you may be to change things for the better, there is always that voice that tells you; will I succeed or will I make a fool of myself? Will the changes be a pleasant surprise for the clients or will I end up shocking myself instead? This is all human. It is unlikely you will avoid butterflies in your tummy if you aim for perfection. The good thing is that with your keenness to do the best and nothing but that, once you get down to the implementation stage, butterflies have no room. Still, you need to know what to look out for in order to allay any fears you may have of doing things right.

Key indicators that you are implementing Lean Six Sigma right:

- The project you pick is a priority to your business

- You appreciate the real demands of the process

- You are basing your decisions on actual reliable data

- You are picking the appropriate Six Sigma tool for every situation

- You are communicating your goals to the stakeholders

- You are communicating your achievements to the stakeholders

- You are evaluating your new process on a regular basis to ensure it is working as per your laid out plan.

This is wonderful! There are clear beacons to show you when you are within the track; so you need not worry. Question is: do vehicles keep within the road just because there are beacons? And the reality is in the negative. Sometimes people get off track even when they know the scope of the track.

What to do when your Six Sigma project hits a hitch

Things can be overwhelming at some stages of the project as not everyone you want support from may be helpful. And sometimes things beyond your control just happen. As the perfectionist that you are (you are a Six Sigma person, aren't you?) your instincts are the try, try again business – not giving up.

But if the worse gets to the worst, do not beat yourself into a pulp. Bring your Project Mentor on board and lay things bare. It is not for nothing most mentors are black belts – actually, Master Black Belts (MBBs). These are people who have been through it and come out shining. So chances are the pitfalls you are encountering will not surprise him or her. And even better, your mentor will have apt solutions that will make you envious and all the more driven.

Chapter 9:
Lean Six Sigma in Government Operations

Do you think governments need Lean Six Sigma? And then you will need to figure out whether this methodology of Lean Six Sigma is even doable within institutions of government. Government is a mammoth institution, isn't it? Actually, in the reality of operation, it is a conglomerate of institutions.

The question of whether this methodology of running organizations can do well, or can even be exercised within government can only be answered when you have a clear understanding of what the methodology entails. And that you know. But just to be sure you remember, think about *lean* and what it represents.

Lean

This is basically a set of working methods that are geared towards identifying and eliminating anything that does not add value to the organization. It is just the same way you get the butcher to trim that fat on the meat that you are not going to cook, anyway, once you get home. Why carry it home?

And what happens in case the butcher does not trim such fat? Well, for one you get to pay for something you do not use – because it gets on the weighing scale, anyway. Then you get to waste your precious energy on some unnecessary weight. And you are yet to talk of the space that the piece of fat takes in your bag. This is the kind of waste that lean curtails.

Is your answer now not obvious? Does the government do well with wastage? Hell, no! Wastage of resources – and they are always scarce – can even bring down a government. How many times have you heard of governments being toppled because of scarcity of necessities? And those placards that begin waving on the streets as preamble to the more serious action of ousting the government leader include sentiments of government waste.

Here are the two categories of lean the government could take:

- Value Stream Mapping (VSM)

- Kaizen Rapid Process

Value Stream Mapping (VSM)

This is simply a way of representing the steps of waste elimination visually. In short, you could have some form of diagram or chart showing the entire process you intend to follow in order to produce the most appropriate product or service, while spending the least of resources.

Example:

What is the cheapest process of hiring senior staff that gets the government the most qualified?

Now, for this category of lean to work well, you need to have two different mappings – one showing the current process, from A to Z; the other showing the process you deem fit in cost cutting and ensuring the best result. So, if you are holding a VSM workshop, your top brass team will have the two scenarios clearly demonstrated. And that makes for good appreciation of the situation and also for better comparison.

Kaizen Rapid Process

Kaizen...? Not originally English; but now, kind of, assimilated in business English. They say language is dynamic; that you cannot but agree; because apparently Kaizen is what brings the point home when you are looking at continuous business improvement. *Kai* – Taking apart; and *Zen* – Making good. Here you get to deal with imperfections as you go along. In Kaizen, the changes are not drastic but rather small and sustained; often incremental.

Now considering that there is no day that you will drive through a gate to one compound housing the government, you can appreciate that different institutions within government can opt for different ways of streamlining their operations for better performance.

Six Sigma in Government

The principles of Six Sigma applied within the private sector where organizations are business oriented will also work well within government. After all, delivery of services cannot be improved to efficiency without analyzing the prevailing weaknesses first. And in our case, there is DMAIC to base our evaluation on. In short, the Lean Six Sigma methodology of running organizations is as good in government just as it is good in business organizations.

Only beware that the greatest mess in government is within administrative processes. They can be painfully slow, and sometimes ineffective.

The administrative waste in government often comes in form of:

- Accumulation of pending work – talk of backlog

- Typographical and factual errors in documents

- Work overlap – work often duplicated

- Paperwork that is redundant – serving no gainful purpose

- Unnecessary process stages

- Long hours of accumulated waiting time

- Movements that can be avoided; purely wasteful

- Unproductive shuffling of paperwork

However, once you modify or even overhaul the existing processes and bring Lean Six Sigma into operation, you end up with government bodies rendering services like they were in business; accounting for every minute of their day and all the inputs that they consume.

This is basically how Lean Six Sigma does in government:

- Rendering great services while drastically reducing the cost of that delivery

- Streamlining and improving operations by increasing their speed; people's agility; and overall efficiency.

- Building a high performance working body that is strong enough for the institution

- Managing assets better; reducing risks and actual losses; while delivering real excellence.

In fact, even when not taking on the whole concept of Lean Six Sigma, some government institutions have already begun to implement some strong principles from this methodology. This is affirmation that excellence is not only being sought on Wall Street. To have a peek at government institutions that have been gearing towards excellence, you could look at the IRS or even the Naval Air Systems Command. Government or business, achieving the best at the least cost is always welcome.

Chapter 10:
Challenges to Anticipate in Lean Six Sigma Implementation

Is it not true that to be forewarned is effectively to be forearmed? In that case, it is easy to appreciate that you can do better when you are aware of the most common problems that people encounter in trying to effect changes. It is even more challenging when these changes are geared towards perfection as often people look at you as a person who exaggerates things. Let us agree that really most people would rather you left them in their comfort zone – even when what they are comfortable in is mediocrity.

Incidentally, a Lean Six Sigma Project is not a one-man show and so you cannot help doing a bit of prodding to such complacent people.

Common Problems in running a Six Sigma Project

Process owner not being too enthusiastic

Such people may tell you they are with you in the whole change business, yet when you arrange for a meeting to chart the way forward they do not avail themselves.

Not being able to identify the real process owner

Some organizations are run so unprofessionally even when they are reasonably big, and without properly defined roles it is difficult to tell with certainty the right person to deal with.

Project Champion not rendering necessary support

If, for instance, you have a Project Champion who was chosen amidst acrimony from some top executives, they may not be exactly motivated.

Friction with different departments

Lack of support from some heads of department is something that leads to frustration of process implementation. Sometimes the daily routine needs to be adjusted, and sometimes downplayed, in order for the Six Sigma project to continue smoothly. Now, if the heads whose departments are affected are not co-operative, bottlenecks are bound to develop.

There not being proper accountability at different stages of the process

Encountering barriers in language

If you have some stakeholders who do not speak your common language, things are bound to go slower than necessary. This is because when working as a team, some things need to be responded to spontaneously to capture the mood of the moment. But with language barrier, all these factors have to be ignored as you get a translator to pass the message both ways.

Having people you need resist change; hence slowing down the project

Lack of support from top management

You are doomed from the onset if the organization's executive are not with you a hundred per cent. Is there really anything you can do without resources authorized by them? Say, cash;

access to company vehicles; exclusive working area; and all that?

Lack of Understanding

Guess what? There are those companies that go for what seems to be in vogue just to be seen as progressive. In fact, some are cases of the executive wanting to impress shareholders. And what does that tell you? That they do not, very likely, comprehend the need for organization assessment as in DMAIC; they cannot visualize how adopting the Lean Six Sigma methodology is going to change the way things work in the company; and even the need for extra resources. In short, you have an executive that is bent on making some cosmetic changes; that is, without really changing the status quo.

Poorly executed plans

It is not enough to have great Six Sigma plans and a great champion. If things are not done smoothly and properly, nothing will fall into place. And the results cannot be great.

Too much focus on the ultimate results

You see, when management tries to focus on the percentage profits they need to see as a result of the Six Sigma projects, it is like saying the end justifies the means. What is wrong with that as long as there are profits gained – are you wondering?

Well, processes are sustainable while other ways of forcing outcomes are not. And the Lean Six Sigma methodology works through sustainable processes. They are measurable and easy to define. So once you use them to succeed, you will be able to replicate them over time. And you need to know that an organization is not termed successful from an assessment of one year. That goes over a span of time.

How to Overcome Common Lean Six Sigma Challenges

Display wins quickly

You may not be a show off, but you have seen the public fall for the person flaunting success from the onset. Do they take time to evaluate chances of that success being short lived? Nay! So flaunt what you have. Let stakeholders begin to see the positive impact of the project the soonest.

In fact, show the impressive results to the top management fast and you see them fall head over heels trying to inquire if you need any more resources – even without you asking. And the rest of the organization begins to talk of the project with pride and a sense of ownership. This is a great boost for you!

Try and create good rapport with all concerned

The thing is: good as you may be, you cannot succeed solo – it is either you and the others or nobody at all. So, the wise; the unwise; the bold; the timid; the cheerful; the grumpy; if you are all in this project, you have got to find a way to work with them smoothly.

If you have never noticed, some people try to sabotage your work just because you do not put them in the loop. It injures their ego and because they have some of those funny personalities, the only way to feel better is to mess you up. So, petty as it maybe – possibly even stupid – you could push this further and make everyone around you feel somehow involved; even those seeing your project through the window (If only you could invoke osmosis here!)

Possibly the ancestors had Six Sigma in mind – in their own language – when they said together we win and divided we fall.

Resolve issues quickly

Can you just get into the habit of visualizing the anxiety on the other end once someone has inquired into something regarding the project? Curb that anxiety by answering the question or responding appropriately the soonest. If that happens to be the product owner, you will be winning his or her confidence. And if that is top management, you will be affirming that they did the right thing to approve of the project. Nobody likes to be kept waiting and you know it.

Achieve impressive results

Do they say something about actions speaking louder than words? Well, nothing beats this than the actual results of the actions. When your project doubles revenues while not increasing costs of operation, you get top dogs in the industry who are head hunting for go-getters narrowing down to you. And how nice it feels to be hired on your terms!

In the meantime, what resources will your own top management withhold? Say nothing. And the whole organization will be so proud to be associated with you and the project and support will be overflowing. There is no better way of reducing challenges of project implementation.

Go easy on IT solutions

While it may be tempting to request for some software upgrade or overhaul, this may not be what you need for quick implementation of your processes. And having that may not necessarily be a panacea for problems of efficiency. So if you can stick to simple solutions as far as IT goes, the fewer challenges you will face.

Make use of your Champion

Have you seen students who will die trying to resolve a problem which their teacher would have dealt with in minutes? Hello! Whom are you trying to impress? And is making impressions as important as succeeding with the project at the end? You are much better off referring to the Project Champion whenever you cannot find a solution amongst team members. That is the reason you have been assigned a Champion – better informed and more experienced than the rest of you.

Ensure you have a project implementing team

This is formed by members of your team who ensure that every activity is going as per plan. In this role, then, they are able to notice problems in a timely manner and to seek remedies the soonest. This way you do not have simple problems escalating to big ones or even getting out of hand.

Have charts to indicate progress

The idea is to have people outside your project know what your team has been up to and to get them appreciating the benefit of having the project work. And what a better way that let them visually follow your progress through score cards or charts? At the end, everyone feels upbeat, and your team particularly feels greatly motivated.

Educate top management first

Even before you get to the small fish, it is the big sharks you need to educate in matters of Lean Six Sigma. They need to appreciate the benefits of the methodology and embrace the concept. In fact, they need to reach a point of being excited about it because that is necessary in order to have them facilitate its successful implementation.

Chapter 11:
Why adopt the Lean Six Sigma Style?

If it is bringing sanity to the working place, and if it is making us all smile all the way to the bank through increased profits that lead to increased perks for the staff and such other good tidings, why not?

In the meantime, do not let fancy terms shake your confidence. We have certainly simplified DMAIC for you and DOWNTIME as well. What we need to add is that you are likely to hear Black Belt in the same breath as Lean Six Sigma and that can be unsettling. It need not make you fret; it does not make this management style any more complex.

So what is this Black Belt in Lean Six Sigma?

Black Belt is only a term used to equate the process of knowledge and competence in implementation to the rankings in Karate. So, just like when you are practicing Karate, being a Black Belt means you are top rated.

That is the reason there was a proposition earlier on in this book that some team members be highly trained in advanced statistics. To be top rated, you need to be trained in implementing the Lean Six Sigma aspects of DMAIC, so that an organization can see tangible results in terms of reduced waste and increased performance after a specified period.

Just for information, there is even certification in this regard. The certificate that shows that organizations can bank on you to help them turn their organizations around and get them reaching their potential is called IASSC; this standing for International Association for Six Sigma Certification. It is actually no mean achievement as you are called upon to score 580 points and above out of a possible 750.

Summary of what Lean Six Sigma helps you achieve:

Develops an effective workforce

Everyone from the most junior employee to the highest of executives develops a feeling of ownership and hence responsibility. Each one of them feels accountable for everything that transpires all the way to the project end.

It enhances efficiency

Since wastage is curtailed, output per employee is higher and better and the organization begins to attract more clients; and business booms.

It drastically cuts down on operational costs

High efficiency is one way of bringing down costs. There is also the aspect of producing output that does not need to be reviewed and modified. Costs also come down whenever loopholes are sealed and pilferage is eliminated.

Revenues shoot up

All the aspects of DMAIC lead to increased revenue. This means that each one of those aspects of management is worth implementing because every organization works towards achieving a huge and consistent flow of revenues.

If you are seeking to identify an organization to emulate in flourishing through Lean Six Sigma, you may wish to look at General Electric; Boeing; Dell; and such other companies that today have a place of prestige in their respective industries.

Chapter 12:
How good is Lean Six Sigma for Small and Medium Size Companies?

How often do you hear the phrase, *it depends,* used? It often implies that there are variables that are not necessarily universal. Do you enjoy ice cream? It depends – yes, on the weather; on the maker; on the social environment you are in – all very subjective. The same case applies to the categorization of organizations as per their sizes. Only here it is safe to say it depends on the country the business is in.

While companies within EU countries pass for being small size when their number of employees does not exceed 255, in the US that number is officially 500. In practice, however, that number can even shoot to 1,500. Anyway, size notwithstanding, your interest is as to whether you can bank on the Lean Six Sigma methodology to turn things around for the better when it comes to business performance. And the straight answer is yes.

And how does Lean Six Sigma help companies that are relatively small?

This actually is not complex. Ask yourself:

- Do you want your handful of employees smoking away their time as they wait for raw materials to arrive, in order to do whatever they are paid to do?

- Would you like remnants of your produce going down in the rot, or reaching expiry date, just because you could not tie production to demand?

- How do you like being kept waiting in the boardroom, say, for an hour anticipating the arrival of other board members?

- How about paying a fully qualified accountant and still outsourcing the accounting function to another firm?

- Do you think it favors your organization to transport your bulky products in small vans or would you rather you cut costs by using trucks?

- How do you feel when you cannot meet your orders? Is it alright just because you call yourself small?

- And does it disturb you to see employees wandering aimlessly within the company?

- And how about trying to produce high standards while continuing to cost services at base rates?

Guess what? If DOWNTIME is not good for the Fortune 500 companies, it is not good for the small and medium size ones either. Just as they say what is good for the goose is good for the gander, here you can wisely say that what is good for the big companies is just as great for the smaller ones.

You want to cut all categories of costs; you want smooth processes; you want to increase revenues; and that is about all that there is to it. You want to be the best that you can be. So, it is your prerogative to go for 99.99966% excellence; and that is, obviously, the Six Sigma level. Paul Keller, a known author, is a great advocate of using Lean Six Sigma in all business sizes.

Are there many small and medium size companies working at Six Sigma level?

Clearly, it is not happening significantly as per now. In actual fact, many are those that operate at between Level 3 and Level 4 at best. And guess how much that effort eats into their revenues? Between 15% and 25% is the proportion of revenues that is consumed just to get each of these organizations operating at that level. Call it the cost of quality. And that is actually not good enough; especially considering there is a better way. Why earn in two or three years what you are capable of earning within a single year?

What is the cost of quality for a Six Sigma Level business?

Believe it or not, but just by moving from Level 4 to Level 6, you can cut your cost of quality to a mere 2% of revenue; or even 1%! No wonder the hike towards perfection makes revenues flow like manna from above!

Incidentally, even when your organization is rather small, you base your operations on the same principles.

- Instead of spending money and other resources fighting fires, you become proactive. Fighting fires...? Sure – like trying to soothe customers breathing fire and brimstone for having received sub-standard goods. Your costs here are failure related – in fact, call them failure costs. And they do you no good.

- You deliberately incur what you can call Prevention Costs. Preventing fire...? Yes, kind of. You prevent failure by being proactive; doing what you need to do to increase your revenues and keep your customers happy.

For example, whatever you do to boost your sales falls under these preventive costs. And, if you recall, we mentioned that Lean Six Sigma is customer centered.

- In both big and small organizations working towards perfection, you get to develop infrastructure at Executive level so as to be able to provide the support needed for the success of the Lean Six Sigma Project.

- DMAIC applies in small companies just as it does in big ones. After all, how are you going to put the right system in place, even assembling the right team, if you do not understand the business scenario as it is before any changes are effected? Are they not hitches you need to identify so as to minimize or eradicate them? After all, moving towards Six Sigma is moving towards minimal errors of operation.

So you define the problems; measure them; analyze them; improve the status; and get to control the whole situation and keep everything on track. That is precisely the DMAIC that works in large companies, and it sure is going to lead smaller companies to excellence. Of course excellence is seen in the final results – the bottom line; but in the process, you will have made stakeholders very happy. Talking of your customers; the shareholders; your employees; and other interested parties.

Ease of implementation of Six Sigma in Smaller Companies

Have you heard something called bureaucracy? Well, maybe not so much these days because many organizations have realized it slows them down. Yet it really is there to some degree or in some form or other; where when you request for a go-ahead you have got to wait for someone above you to ask another who is above her and that one asks another one above him. And by the time you receive a response, it is actually irrelevant because if it was initially on a leaking roof it has now added rotten wood and falling gutters to the problem.

- Small organizations are fast in decision making

- Employees often do overlapping duties and so they appreciate the relationship between one function and the others. This then makes the understanding of the select Six Sigma project much easier for employees involved than in a big company when there tends to be too much specialization and what economists term division of labor.

- You may not need to have numerous Six Sigma projects in a small company. And, of course, the fewer the projects the more convenient it is to run monitor and implement them.

Chapter 13:
How to Embark on Implementing Lean Six Sigma

Ever heard someone warn that saying the ram is fat is no proposition that it be slaughtered? If you have not, no worries – in any case, that saying is organically African. But here, you would not be exercising prudence if you let a good system go untried. You have seen that Lean Six Sigma cuts operation costs drastically; involves virtually every team member thus making everyone feel valued; makes revenue figures somersault eliciting wide smiles from shareholders; and basically makes everyone happy. Why then would anyone with this valuable information not embark on implementing it? Please say you are not too mesmerized to begin.

Identify a Champion

Champion...? Well, a champion leads, right? And here in Lean Six Sigma you are looking to building a team. You are also looking to soliciting resources. There is also the building of some kind of working structure – call it even your modus operandi (*Let them know you know some Latin, why not? Or some legal jargon...*). Anyway, all these fundamentals need someone to structure how they are going to happen. And hence the need for this Project Champion.

When to bring in the Project Champion

The Project Champion is the one to take the project from the ground. So you need him or her like yesterday. In fact, even before you know what shape the Lean Six Sigma project is going to take, it is important that you have this guy. If there is anyone to pull hairs to baldness, it is the project champion – convincing top management that the project is worth the paper it is outlined on; and even laying its groundwork. In fact, do not lose sight of the grim reality that some organizations still have those old guards – wise alright – but still with the 18th century thinking. And without their signatures on the check you are not going to get any funds.

The Basic Role of the Project Champion

Coming up with the project

You know if you come up with a project that gets stakeholders wondering if your organization has been bought out you will be digging your own grave. So the project champion needs to be able to come up with a project that is relevant to the operations of the organization. A project that draws attention to the organization's increased efficiency rather than superficial changes is what you want.

Gauging your project against your organization's strategic objectives

After all the good work of sourcing materials and engaging everyone in cost cutting is done, you need to emerge from the same end of the tunnel that the organization envisaged long before your project came to being. If, for instance, the organization looks forward to serving the region in 5yrs, you need to have that in the picture even as you improve efficiency. In short, you could be termed unsuccessful if you attained 98% efficiency but ended up serving only your country by that time.

Liaise with the very top

For every penny that gets out of the organization's bank account, the top leadership must give their blessings. That goes for other major decisions like altering employees' working schedules and so on. That is mainly why you need to have a project manager who does not freeze in the presence of the big guys and who also does not have a tendency to grow horns when given important responsibilities.

Pinpoint key project personnel

- The Project Lead

- Project Finance Certifier

I hope that tells you outright that the Project Champion is not the guy for the dirty work. Challenging, yes – bumping onto each other with regular team members on a day-to-day basis, no. And even the sensitive role of saying the team is justified to request this and to spend that the Champion delegates to someone else.

This underlines the importance of the Champion's role; being able to observe the overall picture of the Six Sigma project. For this reason, it is presumed that the Champion is capable and willing to appoint the two main officers for their competence and competence alone. Obviously, anything with the semblance of biases or prejudices being a factor would be jeopardizing the success of the project.

Analyzing Project Performance

Of course, you must remember reading that the project is assessed periodically. Now the person to give the project the green light to proceed to the next stage is the Project Champion. If, for any reason, he feels dissatisfied with your product at that stage, then the relevant parts would have to be redone. And if it is to do with provision of a service, even that would be reviewed and if farmhands have to be replaced, then that would happen.

Whereas the Project Champion may come across as the boss with both hands in the pocket, his is not such an easy job. To be a Project Champion comes with great responsibility because at the end of the project, the buck stops with him or her. However, seeing a Lean Six Sigma project to its successful completion is an additional feather to the Champion's hat; a real boost to the Champions resume.

Who Qualifies For The Position Of Six Sigma Project Champion?

Me! Me! Oh, no. This position is not filled in a haphazard manner. Just like the Champion is expected to be diligent when appointing a Finance Certifier, so is anyone in top management when it comes to supporting someone for the role of Project Champion. This is not one of those offices where you sit and rock the chair all day long waiting to append your signature onto something that nobody will ever inquire about. So, here are the criteria:

Be part of senior management

Do you know the reason?

- It is unlikely that you left college and found yourself in a senior management position. So, naturally, you have gone through muck to get to where you are. You have, for example, witnessed firsthand the reality of employees being all smiles today and tomorrow they have placards with your name on it – and in negative light, for that matter. Having survived such challenges, you now know how to run a team.

- Your time climbing up the ladder has given you great experience that is necessary for such changes that would be seen to be radical.

- Being one with the top management puts you in good stead when it comes to lobbying for resources.

Having held a similar position before

Obviously, if you can truly say, been there and done that, you are very well placed. You know what challenges to anticipate, which means you can put measures in place to cushion your project and your team; you have an idea how resources become necessary along the way as incidental costs and hence you can provide for them; you are aware how tight employees schedules can become a handicap and so you can psyche the top management to expect requests for flexible working hours; and so on.

A bonus if you have been a Project Lead before

You see theory and practical are two different realities. Please... Isn't that really obvious? Maybe; but in some areas, once you know the theory the practical part is a smooth ride. But there are positions like this one of Project Lead that you may not exactly understand until you enter those shoes.

At times you may find yourself dealing with clients who like giving verbal specifications and you are not worried because you scribble down as they speak. But then the danger is that they have no qualms denying those specifications when the product is finally complete. And they make you look bad. Not to mention you have to face the reality of the organization losing resources on your watch. How can you empathize with your Project Lead unless you have been in such a situation yourself? How would you bring yourself to tone down criticism on your Project Lead when team members fail to attend meetings having been derailed by their department heads?

Yet for there to be a healthy working atmosphere, empathy and support are necessary amongst team members; between the Project Champion and the team; between the Lead and team members; between the team and the client; and even between the Project Champion and his appointed assistants – the Project Lead and the Finance Certifier. In fact, it can be very frustrating, for example, for the Project Champion to trash particular demands for funds just because of the timing, without understanding that it is very difficult to anticipate all expenses.

Be aware of the tools to measure quality

How else would one tell if the quality has been met unless with clear knowledge of the relevant tools of assessment?

Be alive to the strategic goals of your organization

Why is this, yet the Project Champion is not becoming the CEO's equal? Well, he or she is not getting any more senior than he or she already is, but then it would hurt the organization to have the Champion working towards divergent goals. Remember that everything happening under the organization should be geared towards achieving the ultimate goals of the organization.

In fact, it is in this light that the Champion will identify the Lean Sigma Project to undertake. The strategic goals will determine too how the Champion lays down the resource allocation structure.

Chapter 14:
Yellow and Green Belt Certification in Lean Six Sigma Training

There is formal training for this methodology? Sure! How else would you get experts certified? You have to learn how to implement Lean Six Sigma; that being after learning the best way to assess existing processes. In any case, an organization would need some documentation to go by when hiring an outsider as a Project Champion, a Project Lead, or simply as a valuable Black Belt.

After training, you can tell if processes require adjustment

Ever heard if it ain't broke don't fix it? I did not say it and neither did you. That warning must have come from the mouth of some streetwise chap who learnt the hard way. So even you, on realizing that your organization is operating at Six Sigma Level Six, let it be. Refrain from disturbing the great flow of well performing processes. After all, Lean Six Sigma is about fixing what is broken; erasing inefficiencies to bring in efficiencies.

Just to recap from points you read earlier on, when you undergo the relevant training, you are assessed and when you score 580 points or more out of 750 points, you receive International Association for Six Sigma Certification (IASSC).

What is the IASSC program all about?

Well, it involves teaching you more or less what you have learnt in this book; but there are some structured classes usually found online. If you want, you may check these out for a boost. You know sometimes it just feels good to be able to share the technical jargon with others as informed as you are. And even when it is not about feeling good, at least you do not want anyone trying to impress you with big or colorful words that mean nothing more than you already know. So you need that information; and the certification too to tell the world what you are capable of handling.

Anyway, in this certification program, they take you through 3 major steps:

1. Lean Six Sigma Yellow Belt

2. Lean Six Sigma Green Belt

3. Lean Six Sigma Black Belt

And so you become like those skilled, highly disciplined and motivated Karate kids.

Lean Six Sigma Yellow Belt

What are you expected to learn here? Or rather what do you gain by this level of training?

- You get to appreciate the whole essence of Lean Six Sigma in an-depth manner

- You get to appreciate what it takes for a project to qualify as high impact improvement

- You get knowledge on establishing apt measurements for Lean Six Sigma processes

- You get prepared to be able to use DMAIC to evaluate and complete Lean Six Sigma projects

Ultimately, you will have grasped the fundamental understanding of things to do with process management, and definitely, process improvement.

How long is this Yellow Belt stage?

- A whole 2 days of conventional training

- Alternatively, you have 4 sessions, each 3hrs long; that is, when taking the course online

On successful completion of the course, you are issued with the IIL Lean Six Sigma Yellow Belt Certification. Please note that IIL stands for International Institute of Learning, Inc.

Is this a course for mathematicians who can do formulas?

Definitely not – you need know no formula to avoid waste. The course will do you good if you are involved or about to be involved in a Lean Six Sigma project. This is one of those courses that do as well as team building; where it matters little that you are an executive or you deliver mail for the team.

As long as you want to learn the basic principles; ideas; and terminologies relating to Lean Six Sigma, this training is for you.

Specifically, what does a Yellow Belt trainee learn?

- The art of establishing a working structure that helps to run the Lean Six Sigma processes and bring forth the required quality

- How to identify worthwhile projects – high impact ones; for Lean Six Sigma; those that are compatible with the strategic goals of the organization

- Mastering effective implementation of DMAIC, by learning how to do proper documentation; measurement; and improvement of main processes.

- Calculating the most important Lean Six Sigma measurements

These are basically:

- The Sigma level – is your organization at 1, 2, 3 or 6?

- The DPMO – which, if you recall, is Defects Per Million units of Output

- Yield – that is, the percentage of success. Hey, it is simple: If you have 300,000 defects out of a million units of overall output, what do you take to be the correct percentage of defects; and what is your percentage yield? Hello! This is no scary binomial reference or such Greek math (me too – never heard of Greek math...). Anyway, these two are complementary. The minute you have one you have the other. In our case here, your percentage of defects is 30% [300000/1 000000] and correspondingly your percentage yield is 70%.

- Using reliable data to make important business decisions

Lean Six Sigma Green Belt

How long is this intermediate phase of training?

Well, it is much longer than the elementary one. This stage covers:

- 8 days of conventional teaching

- Alternatively, 16 sessions, each of which is 3hr long; when you are studying online. Gladly, the sessions are well spaced out to cover a span of 2mths.

Who qualifies to undergo this Green Belt training?

Considering that it is more advanced than the basic level that is Yellow, the preference is, understandably, people with a higher level of understanding of the Lean Six Sigma outlook. These include:

- Process experts

- Members of Lean Six Sigma projects

- People looking forward to actually leading relatively small projects

- People looking forward to collecting relevant data for Black Belts

- Anyone anticipating a leadership role in an organization

This stage happens to be the intermediate level of the Lean Six Sigma training; and to get here, it means you are comfortable with the basics of the methodology. Of course, you know the specifics we are talking about here – being able to tell how badly the existing processes are, for one, and how well you plan the replacement processes to be – and all data based.

Here, you will go a notch higher; sometimes a little deeper. You will, definitely, be reminded how to properly identify high impact projects; and also how to align your processes to the organization's long term goals. You will then have plenty of additions to learn, including:

- How to make an elaborate plan for a Lean Six Sigma project

- How to identify and clearly articulate the needs of your customer – they call them CTQs sometimes

- How to objectively analyze data

- How to assess the capability of the chosen process

- How to lay your hands on the actual underlying problems that exist; those that make the organization operate at a low sigma level

- How to properly implement recommended changes which are meant to improve the new or modified processes

- What to do to ensure that the gains are sustained

And guess what makes learning at this stage relatively easy?

Well, you can summarize it by the word *practical.*

- The lessons are interactive and so that means you will have gained confidence in playing your role by the time the course is over

- Your instructor gives you exercises that provide you with hands on experience

- The instructor even uses simulations. That being a very visual teaching method, it is not easy to forget what you learn. And grasping the reality is also relatively easy.

At the end of the day, you will have mastered how to apply the techniques of Lean Six Sigma in organizations of different sizes; how to identify the root causes of defects within the existing systems and processes; and even how to use the Lean Six Sigma tools to alleviate those defects.

What will you achieve by the end of the course?

- Definitely, you will get the IIL Lean Six Sigma Green Belt Certification

- You will be capable of comfortably implementing the processes of DMAIC

- You will be capable of taking a lead position where Lean Six Sigma projects are concerned

Chapter 15:
Black Belt Level of Certification within Lean Six Sigma

Is this the stage at which everyone expects your performance to bring forth head turning results? Simply yes – organizations looking to overhaul their processes and adopt the Lean Six Sigma methodology will seek you out. And your organization will seek to get you involved in the identification and implementation of relevant projects. The course is informative, valuable, and says something weighty about your abilities.

Lean Six Sigma Black Belt happens to be the most advanced level in this 3-part training.

Effectively, how long does the Black Belt course take?

- 8 days of traditional, or you can say, conventional training

- Alternatively, you take a course online that takes you through 16 sessions, each of them 3hrs long.

Who is qualified to undergo this training?

This one is an easy guess. Nobody climbs a tree from the top; and considering that this stage is the most advanced of the three, you naturally need to be someone already certified at the lower level. So you need to have a Green Belt already in order to fit in the Black Belt class.

And what do you learn at this Black Belt stage?

Well, you get to learn the remaining of what there is to learn in handling the Lean Six Sigma methodology. Whatever they did not teach you as a Green Belt will be incorporated in the material for the Black Belt. Specifically, however, your training focus at this stage is on:

- A significantly high level of statistical analysis

- How to manage organizational change

At the end of the day, you will be comfortable analyzing data; identifying the underlying causes of defects; and putting in place optimal processes.

- In fact, the course demands that you identify an organization within your local area and undertake a Lean Six Sigma project; which is beneficial to you and as well as to your chosen organization because:

  o You get to increase your hands on experience, which makes you not just more competent but also more confident

  o It raises that organization's Return On Investment (ROI); which is what all companies are striving to do

Specifics of what you learn at the Black Belt stage:

- You learn how to use statistical software for precision in managing the project – specifically, the Minitab package

- You learn the best strategies in sampling, including the most reliable sample sizes; and also the important aspect of confidence levels

- You learn how to determine the capability of a process, both on a short term basis as well as long term

- You learn how to compute yield metrics; hence being able to evaluate effect of modified processes; level of waste within individual processes; and such other related assessments

- You learn how to develop control charts

- You learn how to analyze existing flow charts

- Mastering how to evaluate the performance level of a system

- You learn how to use hypothesis tests in the comparison of different measurements, including means; variance; and even proportions

- Handling analyses of regression and all other evaluations, including residual

- Doing experiments involving deep analysis and also of process design

Wow! This is high level stuff that leaves you familiar with all aspects of Lean Six Sigma starting from the due diligence level to the place where Return on Investment screams the project success.

Any higher you can go as a Black Belt?

Well, there is actually another feather that you could have added onto your hat, and that comes from your peers. What gives it even more credibility is the fact that there is a standard; you get to sit an exam.

Master Black Belt Certification

Who handles this very high level of certification?

Well, this is done by the American Society for Quality, commonly referred to as ASQ. And the significance of this certification cannot be overstated.

- It underlines your excellence in all matters pertaining to Lean Six Sigma

- It announces to the world of those seeking excellence that your expertise is sharp and refined

- It is an indicator of your deep knowledge in matters of excellence

- It is also a pointer that your own competence in matters of leadership is outstanding

- It says that you are innovative

- It shows that you drive processes to quality single mindedly and that you are among the best when it comes to improving processes.

Who can get this title?

As with every other certification denoting excellence within Six Sigma, you have got to sit relevant exams. And not everyone can do these exams.

For the purpose of eligibility:

- You need to be already practicing as a Master Black Belt (MBB) in your current organization

- You are fine if you already are qualified for Six Sigma Black Belt (SSBB)

Above that it is important that you fulfill one of the following:

- Your experience as a practicing SSBB or MBB should reach 5yrs

- You need to have completed a minimum of 10 Six Sigma projects strictly as a Black Belt

As you can recall, certification at this level must have the blessings of your peers. In this regard, therefore, you get your credentials and your entire portfolio reviewed by a set panel before you get the green light to proceed to sit the MBB exam.

And what kind of portfolio is good enough for MBB certification?

- You must show proof that you are capable of teaching

- Prove you are capable of coaching

- Show you are capable of mentoring

- Show proof that you have occupation related experience

- Showing proof of having held positions of high responsibility in your occupation

- Show that you can have technical experience; that is not just theoretical

- Show you are capable of being innovative

Whatever you present, that panel that comprises your MBB peers evaluates it for relevance and appropriateness of your material; and also its quality.

How is the MBB Exam?

Serious business it is. You get to take the exam in two sessions and each of those sessions is 2½hrs long.

- 1st Part: Here you answer 100 multiple choice questions from here to everywhere; anything you could come across in a work environment

- 2nd Part: This one that also takes its 2½hrs is relatively specific; assessing how well you understand the knowledge content already taught at this MBB level. You can, for instance, be given materials relevant to a particular situation and then you are asked to do your own evaluation and also give what you deem your best response to the specific situation.

This very important examination is normally conducted two times in a year – within March and also October.

After compiling your portfolio and successfully going through the review; and after passing the MBB exam, you can now heave a sigh of relief as you are now due for the most prestigious certification in this area – the Master Black Belt Certification.

Chapter 16:
How does Six Sigma Compare to Total Quality Management?

Six Sigma increases quality and that is a fact. Total quality is also about raising quality and that is also a fact. Do those two facts qualify to have an equal sign between them? No; Six Sigma is not the same as Total Quality Management (TQM). And this is why:

- TQM develops systems; deploys them; and maintains them.

- In this method, quality improves on a gradual basis.

- Six Sigma is geared towards shaping a culture in which the various departments liaise to drive the organization's goals

- When it comes to Six Sigma, it does not address behavioral change; it is more statistical.

- It focuses on measurable performance and means of improving that performance.

- Beyond aiming at quality as well as working with statistics for accuracy and decision making, Six Sigma comes with the dimension of cutting down on waste.

- Six Sigma is not like the ruthless cost cutting processes that also tend to take away a big chunk of quality. It just gets rid of waste; not cutting absolute expenditure.

In summary, this is how different Six Sigma is from the traditional method of improving quality:

- Six Sigma leans towards reducing the occurrence of defects in the relevant sector

- It also leans towards bringing down cycle time – meaning that the customer is served faster

- It is also geared towards cutting all expenditure that is redundant; duplication; or even serving no valuable purpose

- It has a great focus on customer satisfaction and involvement

- Every decision made is based on data and facts

- Results at every stage and in every sector is verifiable in quantitative measure

- Six Sigma is very strategic; having a clear focus from the onset

- In its implementation, it is a Top-Down way of working. This is evident from the hierarchical guidance of the Black Belts; down to the rest of the team members.

- Six Sigma is suitable and implementable in all sectors; including in administration; sales; marketing; research and development; and so on.

If you take each of these three aspects and scrutinize it, you will appreciate that ultimately it ends up having a positive impact on revenues. So, Six Sigma ends up saving the organization unnecessary expenses; raising its quality of output and efficiency of processes; and ultimately increasing its net profits.

And over time, the respective organizations get to develop a culture of efficiency, where everyone is almost allergic to wastage in whatever form. That is great for maintenance of high standards of performance and keeping the organization among the leading ones in the industry.

Chapter 17:
Details of Waste Eliminated By Lean Six Sigma

You know when words are mentioned loosely, you may find it difficult to put your finger on the exact point that needs rectification. Sometimes too, a word may not be mentioned loosely, but if it is left to embrace a whole spectrum of issues, you may find it difficult even then to know which point of your process needs rectifying. That is the same case when you deal with waste in Lean Six Sigma. Of course it is good to get rid of waste, or at least minimize it; but where does this waste come from? What constitutes waste?

Well, let us make it easy for you to remember the different types of waste within the scope of Lean Six Sigma. The acronym to help you is TIM WOODS. This here is not the name of a famous forester, but short for:

Transport

How many times have you seen people moving along an office corridor with files and you thought – well, this is indoors but it really looks like a street busy with human traffic?

Surely, the five minutes you spend delivering a file up seven floors or even to a desk on the other end of your office could be spent better with you doing something that adds real value to your customer. The same case applies to moving products and delivering information.

- Why spend eternity trying to catch someone on phone when you could conveniently and effectively write them an email?

- Why not put your information on soft copy and send as attachments to respective persons instead of delivering the hard copies on foot?

So as you can see, you can cause wastage even when your intents are good but your method of transportation is archaic and unnecessary.

Inventory

Storing inventory is a good idea so that you always have your supplies ready when you need them for processing. However, if you store things that you will only need next season, you will be occupying space that could be better utilized. Look at any space occupied by inventory as accumulating storage costs. Do you really want unwarranted costs? Such unnecessary storage of inventory prior to usage does not just touch on raw materials but also documents; spare parts; as well as other bits and pieces.

Motion

Sometimes there is unnecessary motion that can cause wastage. In a product line, for instance, why not have your employees stand in line if they are doing the same process, so that there is smooth handing over of a product or task? You do not want employees, for instance, doing unnecessary bending or turning; stretching out to reach for items; or even doing lifting that can be avoided.

Waiting

Who wants to sit and wait for the arrival of spare parts from wherever it is while seated idly because the machine has broken down or some nuts have gone loose? Does that not constitute waste in very many dimensions? Wasted hours whose wages are paid; elongated processing time; delayed delivery of final product; and so on. For that matter, when working within Lean Six Sigma, you strive to minimize or even eradicate the need to wait for machine parts and other equipment; instructions; and even information.

Overproduction

Why would you want to produce a couple of tones of goods when the customers' orders only make up one ton? That seems like something you do to satisfy yourself psychologically and not something you do for economic reasons. For one, you will be creating unnecessary concerns of storage and obsolescence.

Over processing

If you add more feathers to the hat than the customer ordered, he or she may just look at you and wonder if you possibly had excessive supply of feathers that you wanted to get rid of. If only two feathers were specified in the order, any more you add do not impress the customer enough for him or her to want to pay more. Likewise when a customer orders Grade 2 of something and you decide to do extra work and apply higher expertise to improve on the product to Grade 1 –that is tantamount to you wasting your resourcefulness and time.

Defects

You do not surely anticipate defects when you are working within the methodology of perfection that is Lean Six Sigma. What you look forward to is perfection or being close to it. So anything you have to rework; anything that is sheer scrap; and even documentation whose information is unreliable; are all categories of defects that add to wastage.

Skills

It is odd how some people embrace too much work while leaving others underutilized. Such underutilized people constitute wasted resources. On the other hand, while delegating can be a great spread out of tasks, you will be laying grounds for waste if you delegate tasks to people without the skills to handle it. To avoid such waste what you do is train the person you want to delegate to on the task in question.

Chapter 18:
Using Lean And Six Sigma above Quality Assurance

Are the principles of quality assurance, Lean and Six Sigma contradictory or complementary? I say, they are complementary and you will observe that reality after analyzing how each one of the aspects works towards the success of your business.

Quality Assurance within a Business

- What does quality assurance entail? It entails taking measures that lead to the production of an item or a service that meets the standards stipulated from the onset. To achieve that:

- You need to document the function that the particular product is expected to perform

- If it is a system, you need to clearly document what that system is expected to fulfill

- You also clearly indicate the resources needed for the process

- At the same time, you ensure that the said resources are actually available

- You need to have specifications for your supplies; that is, to have your intended inputs clearly specified

- It is imperative that qualifications of the people handling the process are spelt out. These are the people who actually make the data based comparison between what is actually happening and what was intended to happen – the people establishing the margin of deviation from the norm or standard.

- There are also situations where quality control involves specifying levels of performance and even output parameters.

Lean

Lean is basically meant to raise efficiency. To raise efficiency under Lean, you need to:

- Minimize waste

- Create a situation where minimum effort is required to succeed

- Pinpoint processes or part of them that do not exactly add value to your business

- Get rid of those steps that are, for all practical purposes, redundant

- Get rid of repeat mistakes, particularly those that consume lots of hours to fix

- Minimize unnecessary movements, whether it be that of products, information, or whatever else

- Bring waiting times down to a minimum

- Work towards making prompt deliveries

- Allocate specific tasks to specific individuals

- Get every person involved to work as per specified guidelines, while taking personal responsibility and hence personal initiative for the task at hand.

Six Sigma

Here is where you work towards minimizing the defects from your processes. And when looking for defects you need to check out the customer's demands first? What are the customer's specifications? If you meet them all, then your product cannot be said to be defective. Do you minimize defects when your quality of work is wanting? Definitely not – so you can already begin to see quality control in the picture here.

Within Six Sigma, the organization goes for simple processes that are smooth enough to produce minimal defects. And they are also simple enough to be carried out by minimal personnel; which means other people can deal with issues in the business arena. Here is where DMAIC generally comes to play – defining; measuring; analyzing; improving as well as controlling.

As you can see, the three aspects of quality control, lean and six sigma, all work towards getting things produced according to specifications. And that is basically the end of story for quality assurance. Yet when you bring in Lean Six Sigma, you notice quality coming forth with efficiency, more so from the lean side of the process. Then you notice that you can actually tell how far off or close you are to certain levels of efficiency – that is the six sigma bit that comes with data based evaluation. In short, for a company that is aiming at coming tops in its industry, quality needs to go hand in hand with Lean Six Sigma.

Chapter 19:
Why Companies Are Not Taking Advantage of Lean Six Sigma

Do you recall the mention that Lean Six Sigma helps companies reduce expenses and thus end up with increased revenues? Well, Praveen Gupta, a consultant who is also an author and who has had occasion to teach matters of business at Illinois Institute of Technology, says that no other methodology of management comes close to creating great savings for an organization like Six Sigma. He says that the amount of savings companies using Six Sigma are making is in the range of billions of dollars.

Of course, as you have already read here, Six Sigma is a management system whose main focus is on customer satisfaction in terms of the appropriateness of products and services that the customer receives. And you also strive to minimize variations in agreed specifications as well as defects. To achieve this, you must be looking at processes that are consistent, and as such, predictable.

Now, when you bring in the strength of Lean to complete the methodology that is Lean Six Sigma, you are bringing in a management arm that is also centrally targeting the customer – using data to determine objectively how close the organization is to meeting the customer's demand and hence to make necessary process adjustments. Here, you look at functions that you want added to your processes but use data to establish if they are worthwhile or not – how worthwhile being a measure of the customer's willingness to pay for that added bit of work. Likewise for the product or service – you check if it is worthwhile adding a certain feature by the willingness of the customer to pay for the extra expense. However, there are some cases when you will not look at the issue from a compensation point of view. Rather, you look at how much of a competitive edge your additional feature or function is likely to give you.

- Does the change result to shortened delivery times?

- Does it lead to decreased costs that allow for a drop in product price?

- Does the adjustment lead to decreased number of defects?

Just to recap then, when you are weighing whether to take up or not to take up Lean Six Sigma in your organization, you need to be aware of the main benefits at stake:

- Improving the quality of products or services

- Improving the customer experience

- Increasing your bottom line

Those were the principle targets of the pioneers of Lean Six Sigma as exemplified by Henry Ford of Ford Motor Company and Taiichi Ohno of Toyota; and they are the same principle targets that continue to guide this methodology as is evidently clear when you consider the case of General Motors and Volkswagen. In fact, Toyota has been consistently on the list of Fortune 500, and a number of times within the Top 10.

Why, then, are some companies still not applying Lean Six Sigma?

Lack of relevant information

Well, for one, this methodology has not penetrated the general market. It is safe to say that it is still with the pace setters. So the reason some companies who would otherwise make huge strides in growth do not even talk about Lean Six Sigma is sheer lack of knowledge. In fact, apart from coming across the term when trying to Google something, or hearing it from word of mouth, there are few other sources of information on this cutting edge methodology.

Believing Lean Six Sigma to be a fad

There are many Doubting Thomases, so to speak, the reason some companies lead while others follow. Some companies that are yet to implement the Lean Six Sigma methodology have heard about it and its advantages. However, often you find CEOs who are close minded and not willing to do anything that seems to challenge the status quo. That is why you find sudden structural overhaul of a company's top management by the board when some forward looking member introduces the idea of change of management style. In short, there are those who dub the relatively new management style a fad simply because of the fear of implementing something new.

Time management that is wanting

Have you ever taken into consideration the fact that time spent, no matter how well or poorly, cannot be salvaged? This, of course, as opposed to an exam failed – you can always do a re-sit. Even a product not well completed – final touches can usually be made later. Anyway, some executives who know about Lean Six Sigma keep it at bay citing lack of adequate time to implement it when really it is a shortcoming in time management.

What such people miss out is the essence of the methodology which is not to become an addition in the organization but rather a modification of the existing methodology; and if necessary, replacement. In any case, if the worry is on the issue of time to train your workforce, there are professionals who are already versed in these matters, as has been indicated before in this book, and they even bear relevant certification. If you hired one of those, they would help you out without the inconvenience of stopping any of your production lines for any significant duration.

The expenses involved in Lean Six Sigma implementation

Do you think you need millions of dollars to begin implementing Lean Six Sigma? No way! In fact, some companies that are not heavily endowed but who happen to appreciate a good thing when they see one have delved into the process of implementing the methodology by giving their key personnel the Yellow Belt training. That is just two days at most. How big, really, is such a cost compared to the doubling and trembling of returns that you are looking at if you implement Lean Six Sigma in full?

Underrating the size of the organization

This business of ours is too small for big methodologies! Do you think you could be too tiny for a fat bank account? If not, how then can you dismiss an improvement tool that does not come as a whole mass but as a combination of implementable principles? If you are small or just medium size but you acknowledge that reducing product defects is worthwhile and you are ready to use reliable data to improve your processes in a way that can be objectively assessed, then you are ready for Lean Six Sigma. In short, you could embrace Lean Six Sigma but implement it in phases. In fact, your most fundamental step no matter the size of your organization is to be able to pinpoint the specific needs of your customer.

Not being involved in manufacturing

Birds fly – fine. Do airplanes fly? Yes, they do as they have what it takes to fly. That is the same case with Lean Six Sigma. Where was it that this methodology was first tried out? In the manufacturing sector – and this was with the likes of Motorola. Does that mean that only the manufacturing sector needs to cut down on losses? And are customers of manufactured products the only ones that need great products? Of course, not! If you want a service, you surely want the best and as per your specifications. And the business enterprise providing the service wants to make as much money as possible by cutting down on costs. In short, there is no business, irrespective of whether it is in the manufacturing sector, the service industry or even trade, that does not wish to be as profitable as it can and to please its customers.

The massive statistics and advanced math

Have you also misconstrued Lean Six Sigma to be all about big math; statistics and probability? Well, it is not. You can still make a big improvement in the success of your business entity without involving yourself with complex figures. Even a business that deals with customer care and not anything like engineering can do with reduction of waste. It can also do with happier customers. Can you identify obvious duplications and redundancies in your organization without holding a calculator or mathematical table? Yes, you can. Can you identify obvious wastage without doing number related calculations? If it is a yes to both questions, then you surely can apply Lean Six Sigma without having to employ a statistician and still reap higher revenues.

Planning to embark on Six Sigma or Lean methodology first

Do you take the two – Six Sigma and Lean – to be mutually exclusive? Of course, they are not. Both Lean and Six Sigma have the customer's satisfaction as their main focus. So you need not delay your endeavor to transform your enterprise as you try to determine which of the two methodologies is best to begin with. That is the main reason you will be talking of Lean Six Sigma projects and not Lean and thereafter Six Sigma down the line or the other way round.

Having tried Lean Six Sigma before and not succeeded

Can you identify the reasons you failed? What, exactly, failed you? Was it the technology you used; the people handling the processes; or the processes themselves?

In short, wisdom lies in you learning from your experience even when that experience involves failure. You fail and then you try yet again – not quit because you once tried and did not make it. In fact, you have great role models in instances of turning failure around to become exemplary success. Think of Henry Ford, he of Ford Motors Company, and the number of times he failed before actually succeeding.

Chapter 20:
Why Lean Six Sigma Is Worth The Effort

Have you thought of a recipe that would be messed up by an extra ounce or two of one or two if its ingredients? Maybe you have not because you consider such precision an unnecessary stress. But guess what? That is part of the reason a product that costs a few dollars being made by certain entrepreneurs costs some tens of dollars when made by another particular entrepreneur.

Customers are sensitive to quality and will pay handsomely for fine stuff. However, you have got to put in the effort to refine your product and make it stand out from the mass in the market. And when you have an order, you have got to make the customer wonder: Why would I go anywhere else? In short, you make your customer's product in such a way that you are leaving no room for someone else to make it better. That is what Lean Six Sigma makes you do – produce the best that could be.

Let us see why else your effort is worth it:

Ability to give your customer best value

You see, as you give your customer the best product he or she could ever get, the customer gets easy on the purse. Customers who understand quality are prepared to pay for it. In any case, you do not add any features and functionalities or anything else whose cost the customer does not foot. So essentially, you are not eating into your revenues while refining the customer's product or service. At the same time, you are making yourself irresistible to the customer in a way that makes the price of the product almost inconsequential.

Can you now not visualize your bottom line growing exponentially? And then you know there is the category of customers who want the best of the best and are willing to pay a fortune for it. With your excellence of production and customer care, such customers will trace your business entity to your doorstep. And it is unlikely you will find a better way to keep in the lead than having customers seek you out even before you go looking.

You have a motivated workforce

If you can recall, it was explained earlier on that the opinion of everyone involved in the Lean Six Sigma project is valued; in fact, encouraged. That in itself is a morale booster. Then there is the feeling of working towards a personal goal, still emanating from the active participation of the employees. And so as they get excited about the success of the project, they also feel accountable for anything that might go off track. For that matter they do their best to ensure everything goes according to plan.

Can you see another plus with this aspect of employees having a positive attitude towards work and feeling enthusiastic about the projects they are involved in? Well, it is indication that the employees are likely to stick with the organization for a decently long time. And as you may know, low employee turnover reflects well on an organization.

Makes the organization adaptable

When you are working with Lean Six Sigma, there is clear data and clear processes. And when it comes to implementation, it is clear who is in charge of what. Every type and amount of input is known to the detail. So whenever something crops up in the market that has a direct impact either on the product or service or even the market itself, your organization can analyze what is happening and promptly make necessary changes to accommodate the new changes. In short, this methodology makes your enterprise strategically placed to handle unanticipated variations in the business environment.

Gives your organization a competitive edge

Are you known for quality? Yes? How about timeliness of delivery? Yes. Adherence to customer specifications...? Yes, that as well. Hearing of you:

- Potential customers will seek you out

- Investors will seek you out

- Vendors will want to deal with your products

Your achievements will be marked by high standards

Excellence is a fundamental factor of Lean Six Sigma. And with this, you get to reap, not just cash rewards but also respectability. That is why marketing agencies are reaping millions to give companies a facelift; to reflect excellence. But with you working with Lean Six Sigma, you do not need to convince anyone that your products or services are worth a try. Excellence in this regard comes with the territory. Achieving excellence in all spheres – production, packaging, delivery and all – becomes easy courtesy of:

- Standardized processes

- Streamlined training of existing personnel

- Simplified project management

- Streamlined monitoring of processes

- Simplified procedures of solving problems

- Having all operations of the organizations streamlined and simple

Provides room for innovation

How can you not be innovative, employing your imagination and creative knack to come up with progressive ideas, when you never have to firefight or strive to do damage control? When you are counting decimals as your degree of failure, as an organization it reflects a scenario where processes are flowing smoothly and where every face is glowing with satisfaction. And you want that for growth, continued stability, and also expansion.

Your bottom line becomes significantly healthy

The reason you are in business is to make profits. Of course Lean Six Sigma is great for non-profit organizations as well, but on this point, businesses are the apt examples. Again, how do you increase the revenues in an exemplary big way?

- Your organization has no longer has waste in their vocabulary and of course that is money saved in that regard

- Your customers are very happy and so they keep making orders and more orders. They do not go anywhere else as you have baited them with your high quality products and services. Increased sales volumes, definitely, translates into greater revenue figures.

- Not many items, if any, delivered to customers are returned. That adds to the element of customer satisfaction and also consistently high sales figures.

Any idea how much a business saves as a result of continued efficiency, courtesy of Lean Six Sigma? Well, reliable sources put the savings to anything between $2,000 per single improvement to $250,000 per such a singular improvement. So you have that size of revenue – savings that would have been lost were it not for the new methodology – and also additional revenues resulting from expanded sales.

And you know what else sends your sales figures skyrocketing? Well:

- Continuously enhancing your reputation

- Expanding goodwill from customers

And did you know that the US army also employs Lean Six Sigma in its operations? Wow! This is a great example of a service group that uses the management method of Lean Six Sigma and ends up making a saving of close to $2 billion!

Chapter 21:
How Do You Write A Business Case For Lean Six Sigma?

When do you spend your money better and find the going smooth – when you have planned your journey or when you have embarked on random travel? Is it when you plan or when you get on with business and do things haphazardly? My bet would be on when you have a plan to rely on. That is the same case when you want to improve your business for the better using Lean Six Sigma. You want to know in advance what the new methodology entails; how much you are likely to spend on the processes; and so on. You need to make a business case for the methodology you want to implement.

The main reasons you want that business case well spelt out are:

- You want to be sure you understand your problem area

- You want to characterize your issues; describing them in a way that is specific and clear

- You can lay out your proposals of how to correct existing problems

- You will be able to lay out the value you expect to gain from your improvement projects

Incidentally, the best way to go about writing down your business case is not to do it alone or to give that responsibility to a single person, whether he or she is a belt holder or not. The most fruitful way is to have your whole team get involved. That task needs to be done in a relaxed environment so you can get authentic details from each member. And it need not be cumbersome. So for starters, give your team members some sticky notes. Around 20 for each individual will do. Of course, whatever they put down will end up on your business writing template.

This is how you describe your problem, just for example:

- Figure for accounts receivables being too high

- Warranty returns being excessive

- Customers not responding well in regard to their orders

- Product costs being too high

- Product yields being too low

Note that as you write down your potential financial benefits, it is important that you rely on data you already have or reliable information that you have.

Here is what you need to include in your business case statement:

- Your nature of business

- Mention of specific problem area

- Mention of your business goal – the target that is adversely affected by the identified problem.

- If there is some other loss or inconvenience being caused by the problem, note it down as well

- Note down the magnitude of your loss in monetary terms and also indicate what period that loss covers

For you to be exhaustive about the problems plaguing your organization, it is worthwhile to tap into the knowledge of the people who are on the ground on a daily basis – your workers. Let each of them work alone for starters, trying to put his or her finger on all the sections they consider problem areas. For each problem area, the employee writes it down on a sticky note as a case idea. Each employee is working independently at this initial stage but thereafter each of them can stick the notes on the wall once he or she has exhausted the organization's areas of weakness known to them. This here is now an opportunity for them to see what everyone else considers problem areas.

Now you want to initiate a Six Sigma project but it has to have a business case. For you to identify that crucial case, you need, together with your employees, to put those similar cases together. That is a way for you to see the business case which is high on the ranking and which then can be given priority.

In sorting these sticky notes and the ideas written on them, you need to have a team leader. From past experience, it has been noted that this exercise brings out around five to ten main problem areas, all suggestions considered. You then compare those selected problem areas and brainstorm on them, giving any fresh ideas any member may have. After adding more flesh in terms of data and information, it is likely that some problem area will emerge higher than all others. That is the case you give priority to and you forthwith identify the person most accustomed with the problem area and you put them in a pivotal role of steering the team.

Benefits of working on business case as a team

The reason a business case is not identified by top management or some hired expert but rather by members of a larger team cross cutting departments is that the organization gets to benefit beyond having the individual problem solved. Here are incidental benefits of employees working together:

- Everyone involved gets to believe in the project

- Each team member develops a sense of ownership of everything discussed and decisions made

- After all sticky notes by individuals are laid out on the wall, the next phase of analyzing them and moving them around to put each in the category it fits best, is very informative for everyone involved. And they get to get a broad perspective of the problems the organization is facing.

- The whole exercise is great for the team members as they bond and get to understand each other better. The kind of relationship created is thus beneficial, not just at personal level, but also at the business level.

For the purpose of selecting your business case, you use a tool called <u>affinity diagram</u>. This is the modified version of gathering and consolidating input from team members in an environment with no inhibitions associated with fear of criticism.

Lean	Safety	Material Handling	Layout Design	Worker Relations	Sanitary Requirements
Standardization missing	Concerns in ergonomics	Issues of raw material transportation	Sourcing of new equipment	Improving employee relations	Improved standards
Mix of products too high	Problem of noise	Issues of material mixing	Cost effectiveness	Improvement of manual operations	Ease of cleaning
Procedures of Loading as well as offloading	Need for preventive measures	Messy handling			Meeting the health code
Packaging Machine outdated	Rate of back injuries	Problems of splashing			Safety of food
Problems of shift changeover	Protection touching on eyes and ears	Handling of heavy material			

Chapter 22:
Summarized Benefits of Lean Six Sigma

As you outline the health quality of a dish, for example, any reason why you cannot pick one ingredient at a time and summarize its health benefits? Likewise, in summarizing the benefits of Lean Six Sigma, you may wish to look at the Six Sigma part on its own and then bring in the Lean part. In any case, Lean Six Sigma is essentially Six Sigma beefed up with better measures.

Six Sigma

Of course, you already know how Six Sigma works with the application of data to improve processes by bringing product or service defects to a minimum – basically only having 3.4 defects occurring in a million times or opportunities. What you need to bear in mind at all times is the two very important elements of this methodology:

- **DMAIC**

- **DMADV**

DMAIC

With DMAIC, you may, of course, recall the Six Sigma arm that deals with processes already in place. And so you define those processes; measure them; do an analysis on them; make improvements on them; and finally, ensure that they are well controlled.

DMADV

This other arm of Six Sigma is the one that deals with processes you want to put in place. They may be processes you want to implement for the very first time in your organization, or they may be processes that you want to put in place to replace others. Either way, DMADV applies; which means that you define that process the way you do with existing ones; you measure it and also analyze it; that essentially making you understand how the process is meant to work and what it is meant to achieve. The last two phases are the ones that differ from the case of existing processes. With a new process, you actually design it and then verify it. That is basically saying that you are doing what needs to be done to put it in working mode; and then you see to it that the process is running as planned.

This is what you stand to gain in your Six Sigma business environment:

You gain more loyalty from customers

You see, with improved processes which lead to fewer defects, what you are saying is that you are making your customers happy almost to the point. And with every customer knowing how difficult it is to reach perfection, your near perfection is more than anyone could ask for. And it is unlikely that such customers would wish to shift to another manufacturer or even service provider. This is how your customer retention level gets to soar. And their loyalty actually gets to draw other people's attention and in many cases pulling them in as new customers. Then you get people wondering how your business seems to be unaffected by increasing competition in your industry – it is that loyalty you have managed to cultivate, courtesy of Lean Six Sigma.

Time is managed better

Did you know that time wastage contributes immensely to final losses? For instance, you get to pay wastages for hours not worked; you get to lose customers just because your employees continue to continue chatting as they sluggishly respond to the customers; and such other uneconomic ways of spending working hours. In fact, you can even trace some product or service defects to poor time management – like wasting so much time that when you get to doing the actual work you are literally rushing it through. How can you surely be thorough and make a product to the customer's satisfaction? You may not even have time to check for quality at different stages!

For great time management, you need to set goals that are dubbed SMART – Specific; Measurable; Attainable; Relevant; as well as Time-bound. Then, of course, you use the data based principles of Six Sigma.

Cycle time significantly reduces

Who wants completion time being pushed by days, then to a couple of weeks, with all the uncertainty and inconvenience that comes with it? As a customer, you want your quantity of products delivered at the indicated time and the products being of the specified quality and all.

Some of the reasons deadlines fail include:

- Unforeseen change of policy

- The scope of the project being adjusted

To circumvent such inconveniences, it is important that the project consists of members of all affected departments as well as members of different employment levels. That means having someone from senior management too who can point out, for instance, when there is a possibility of policy changes or something that drastic. Businesses that manage to constitute their team membership reasonably have a chance of identifying a potential hitch and pre-emptying it. Such businesses have managed to reduce their cycle time by an impressive 35%.

You have a motivated workforce

Do not imagine that workers keep smiling when they are sweating it out for nothing. They will do that when they know that they are being appreciated. And why are they being appreciated? Because under Six Sigma they are producing results that are pleasing to the customer and thus prompting the customers to place more orders. As a result revenues are increasing without the counter effect of returned defective goods. Of course, as you may recall, Lean Six Sigma is one interactive methodology where everyone involved has a say. That in itself has been seen to raise productivity to a range within 25 and 50 per cent.

Facilitating Strategic Planning

In the process of evaluating systems, you get to understand the weaknesses therein as well as the system's strong points. That then helps you identify areas that need modification in order to meet the standards envisaged in the implementation of Lean Six Sigma.

Enabling better management of your supply chain

Just imagine a scenario where you have a supplier for every component of a particular product with multiple parts! You would have just as many people to depend on for the efficiency of your process. This is because delayed deliveries can affect your working process in an adverse manner, just as defective supplies can. However, with lean six sigma, what you strive to do is reduce your number of suppliers. If you analyze the whole scenario further, you will realize that not only will you reduce DOWNTIME, but you will also have a chance to negotiate more favorable credit terms for your organization.

In essence then, your streamlining of the supply system ends up reducing or even eliminating bottlenecks in your processes; reducing the number of defects; and increasing efficiency on the overall. That can only lead your business to its full time objective of keeping costs to a minimum while increasing revenues. What does that equal to in terms of business success? Obviously, a rise in your bottom that is also consistently steady.

And now the arm of Lean within Lean Six Sigma – what are its obvious benefits?

Smooth processes

These smooth processes result in increased speed and accuracy. Can we not just call that faster processing and increased efficiency? And, of course, those are the aspects that most customers consider when thinking of whether to stick with you or go searching elsewhere. In this working environment, the resources you need to put in are always on the decline and that is because the idea of waste is almost superficial now. And with happy customers keeping their accounts running, the revenue side keeps getting heavier. On the overall, your organization then begins and continues to stand out in profitability.

Decreasing costs

This point does not just embrace decreasing costs resulting from reduced waste. Rather, it also includes the reduction of costs that come about when you do tasks that are not necessary; or even excessive processing. Doing any additional task that the customer did not order and even pay for is an unnecessary cost on your side. Gladly, Lean Six Sigma has no room for that kind of redundant tasks.

Increasing Efficiency

Some of these benefits may overlap, but they are also benefits that you can singularly identify. The efficiency of your processes is the one that helps you deliver great products to your customers. Those satisfied customers then endeavor to make prompts payment because your exactness in regards to product or service specifications is impressive and motivating. And so, what Lean Six Sigma provides you is a customer base that is steadily growing, and revenues that are consistently increasing. Where else can a business such as yours look after that but towards expansion? And so if you were small size you turn medium and so on.

Needless to say, this steady growth comes with increased economic benefits; including better credit facilities; economies of scale both in procurement of supplies and delivery of final product.

Developing an effective workforce

Did you know that a lot of hours are lost at the place of work as employees await the so called 'orders from above'? When using Lean Six Sigma, nobody dictates to anybody. How can it happen when everyone was part of the team that laid things on the table; identified existing weaknesses and prescribed solutions? So within this methodology, each person feels accountable and responsible for the success of the Lean Six Sigma project. Each person feels the importance of their role and they work towards its success. In fact, each person understands that his or her role in the whole process will be measured for efficiency even as the overall success of the project is evaluated.

Conclusion

Now that you understand what the Lean Six Sigma method of management is, you can start living it every day. Start with implementing the various aspects of waste reduction. As you get all the respective aspects of process improvement working, you will see a definite change for the better on the overall performance of your organization. Wastage will be a thing of the past; or it will, at least, be reduced to negligible levels. And since waste constitutes a big part that eats into revenues, your bottom line will automatically shoot to impressive levels.

There is also the aspect of problem solving that you have learnt in the form of DMAIC. As you embark on practicing those systematic steps of problem solving, your processes will be improving and your revenues will be increasing as a consequence. That will show you that, evidently, cutting waste and solving problems in the way prescribed by the Lean Six Sigma approach gives fast and progressive results. And you will also see the benefit of having more of your people trained in matters relevant to Lean Six Sigma.

The next step is to go back over the book as needed. At the same time, observe the systems existing in your organization and see where they require modifying. Once you take those initial baby steps leading to more efficient processes, you can easily change your employees' old mindset and help them adopt a new one where they feel in-charge and accountable for their actions. That, in turn, means that they will revel at the success of the organization. What this effectively does is give you a motivated workforce that is eager to save costs for the organization while doing everything to make the organization succeed and beat competitors.

With this powerful knowledge, the ball is now in your court. Work towards helping your organization reach its potential and do not hesitate to congratulate yourself for a job well done when you are finally the leading light in your industry!

PRIVATE LABEL SELLING

Best Proven Techniques And Tips For Profiting From Amazon And eBay Private Label Sales Using Psychical Products !

G. Harver

Table of Contents

Introduction

Private label selling is becoming an increasingly popular way to make money online. Now that it's become more popular, there are many more suppliers to choose from with a variety of products that you can resell. However, there are some things that you need to look out for when you're trying to find a product, and when you're dealing with a supplier.

For example, let's say you've found a product from a supplier you really like, and you believe it will really sell. You order a bulk order without ordering samples first, and then you get a phone call or a message from a lawyer who tells you that you've ordered a knock-off item that is illegal to sell in the United States, or in whatever country you live in. You've lost the money you sent to the supplier, and you've lost the products because they're going to be confiscated. You don't want to end up in that situation, so how do you know what you're dealing with?

Look for the answers in this book.

You'll find information pertaining to how to find a good product and tell a good product from a bad one. How to find a supplier and build a relationship with them, and then how to sell the product once you receive it. You'll also find information on how to move forward with your sales, and some answers to frequently asked questions that are common in the industry.

So keep reading for some great information!

Chapter 1:
What is Private Label Selling?

Private label selling is purchasing a product that is able to be relabeled and packaged under your company or brand name. You are essentially remarketing a product that is already being made by the manufacturer for your purposes. An example of this might be when you go to the grocery store. Say you really like a brand name, and then you pick up the store brand's packaging and begin to read the ingredients. If they're the exact same and the nutritional information is the same, the store most likely purchased their product from the same manufacturer who made the brand name's product.

Therefore, instead of having to manufacture a product yourself, you can purchase the products at a low cost and assign a label and brand that's yours, and then resell them to the public for a higher price in order to gain a profit.

So what are the benefits of selling a private label product?

No Manufacturing

Instead of having to manufacture an item, you get to purchase it. There are numerous assumptions that private labeling is not going to sell a product, but there is a view that if you sell a product, you have to manufacture or make it yourself. That is not the case anymore. You are able to sell a product under your own brand and still sell plenty of that product. In addition, you don't have to think about changing or modifying the products you purchase as selling them is more fruitful.

Modifications

However, if you do want to modify the product, you are able to do so with private labeling rights. You are able to modify any product you purchase before you sell it, and that's a lot simpler than having to think of a new product from scratch. The usual rights for reselling do not allow you to modify a product before you sell it, but if you have a new idea that you think you can turn your product into with private labeling, you can use the new idea and make the product's position in the market more advantageous. Once you purchase private labeling rights, the product is yours.

Customer Demand

You're able to satisfy customer demand because you don't have to think about a new concept for a new product anymore. And if you try doing that, another company could beat you to the punchline and they're selling as you're still innovating. Therefore, you can sell and sell through private labeling and avoid the hassle of having to be innovative. You just purchase the product, brand it with your name and label, and sell it as if it's your own.

No Variance

Thinking of a new product can be dangerous. It may either flop or it can become a hit. The variance is too high for thinking up a new product. In the competitive selling environment, trial and error can become so costly that you fail. However, if you purchase a private label product, you already have a customer base and then you can just sell them. You just have to be great at marketing.

41426010R00075

Made in the USA
Middletown, DE
12 March 2017